Dear Debra,

Wow ... such
an involved and
caring mom!
How super!

Continue to
embrace life with
joy, love and caring.

With best wishes,

Judy Cohen

From the Guidance Counselor's Office

By

Judy Cohen

authorHOUSE

1663 LIBERTY DRIVE, SUITE 200
BLOOMINGTON, INDIANA 47403
(800) 839-8640
www.authorhouse.com

First published by AuthorHouse 06/18/04

ISBN: 1-4184-8114-9 (e)
ISBN: 1-4184-2823-X (sc)

Printed in the United States of America
Bloomington, Indiana

This book is printed on acid-free paper.

I dedicate my book with love to my students, the high school staff, my sons, their wives, my grandchildren, and my husband. All have enriched my life and for this I am forever grateful.

Table of Contents

Choices

Depression, Grieving, Healing

Scholastic Success

Holiday Musings

Conclusion

Introduction

I have been a guidance counselor and an educator for over twenty years and have gained so much from my students and their parents. I have listened, I have shared, I have cared and through all of this I have learned. Issues have been aired, solutions have been sought and growth has occurred, not only growth for my students, but growth for me, too. Together we have come up with solutions. Some have worked; some haven't. But at least we moved forward.

Many parents have asked me to put together a book concerning the happenings that have transpired in my office and the wisdom and lessons that have been learned. It is my hope that others will gain insight from my observations and suggestions. Perhaps they will come up with ideas of their own that will work even better. No issue has a single solution. I have learned that what works for one person does not work for another person. I have learned that it is important to be flexible and willing to change.

I decided to divide my book into various chapters dealing with themes. Some vignettes could fit into several themes; however, I have tried to include them in the most appropriate ones. Within each chapter are stories that are based on fact, yet the names of the players have been changed. Also included are articles based on ideas that I have learned through life's experiences.

Hopefully you, the reader, will not only find these stories interesting, but also you will be able to relate to them. If they have some positive impact on your life, I will have succeeded in my purpose for compiling this book, for what better legacy is there than to have touched a life and made it better?

Parenting Issues

The hardest job in the world is being a parent…and it's the most important one.

Communication Tips for Parents

Communication is a five-syllable word with so much packed into it. According to the dictionary, communication is a process by which information is shared between people. Communication needs a sender and a receiver. You can speak aloud, but if no one hears you, what good is it? Of course, sometimes as a parent, you speak to your youngster, you have a receiver, but you really don't feel you are heard at all!!

Think about the word communication. Without it, where would we be? How would we make our wants known? How could we express anger, fear or love? How could we understand others' desires? How could we share with others, learn from them or help them? How could we develop and grow?

Since the communication process is so important, I have listed some useful tips to facilitate the process. The tips do work, so give them a try and watch your communication skills soar! You'll be amazed at what you learn about your kids in the process.

1. Teach your child to listen. Look him in the eye when you talk; this should help to hold his attention.

2. Speak in a quiet voice; if you yell, he will yell. Shouting shuts down listening skills; normal tones enhance them.

3. If your child is much smaller than you, bend down so you will be at his level. This is so less intimidating.

4. Practice not only listening, but also talking. Include your child in conversation. In this way, you will make him feel important and by engaging him in conversation, you will be helping him to communicate.

5. Use courteous words; if you use profanity, so will your child. A child learns by example.

6. Invite more comments by giving short answers such as "I see", "Tell me more," "Really," and other words that show you are paying attention but not usurping the conversation.

7. Praise your child with some encouraging words as he speaks; this makes your child feel good and lets him know that his message is important.

8. Avoid giving negative responses; they stifle conversation.

9. When your child speaks, give your undivided attention. Don't watch TV or do other tasks. Otherwise, how can you expect your child to listen to you?

10. Sometimes talk to your child one on one, away from other members of your family. Give him time alone with you to discuss things.

11. Listen, speak and share. It's amazing what you will learn.

***

Instruct or Destruct

Did you ever feel like tearing your hair out? Of course you have. What parent hasn't, for we all know that parenting is probably the hardest job we will ever do in our lives and the irony is that it really doesn't come with instructions. Yes, there are books written, but there are really no set rules to parenting. There are guidelines, there is common sense and of course there is winging it, which is what most of us tend to do anyway.

When I look back at my parenting, I realize how far I have come. Frankly, there should never be first children; the poor souls…they are the ones who are the guinea pigs; they are the ones on whom we dauntingly try out our skills. From them we learn, sometimes the hard way, and definitely through trial and error, what works and want doesn't. Yet, here's the problem, when the second kid arrives and we try to use some of the same learned tools, they just don't seem to work. And why is that? I think it's because each kid and each situation is so unique. But there does seem to be one constant and that's what I wish to address. The constant is our demeanor, our behavior. We must instruct, not destruct.

Let's think about both of these words. It is important for us to instruct our children, to show them by example what is the appropriate thing to do. It is important for us to tell them why we feel they are doing the incorrect thing or why they are acting in an appropriate manner. We must listen to them, but as parents, we must remember that we do have and should have permission to instruct. We are their teachers. And just as a good teacher does, we must lead the way and do it in a constructive fashion. Yes. That's the key…we must instruct positively.

Now, let's look at the word destruct. Unfortunately, that word is invoked much too frequently. I like to think it's done unknowingly, yet it is so damaging. John's room is a mess. You are tired of telling him to pick up his things. This time

3

you enter his room and start yelling, telling him to respect you and that his room is part of your home. How dare he not clean it! You go on to tell him that he is a slob and you are sure that's why he is getting low grades in school. Whoa! Wait a minute! How did school enter into it? What do low grades have to do with his room? Clearly you have let things get out of hand. You are angry and are spouting forth things that are inappropriate and are just being destructive. And you know what? You are turning Johnny off. A matter of fact, he has probably tuned you out at this point, saying to himself, "Here she goes again."

Okay, so what should you have done? Let's take a look. You enter his room.

You say quietly and evenly, "Hey, kiddo, I see things haven't gotten picked up yet. What's the story? Do you have enough room for everything? Were you too busy to straighten up?"

Give Johnny a chance to respond. You might be surprised what you hear. Then, begin to instruct, not destruct.

"Johnny, let's clean this place up together. I don't want to put your things away into places where you won't find them. Got any suggestions?"

Now you are both in this together. He is helping you and you are helping him. Once the room is straightened up, point out to him what a difference it makes. You are not only pleased at the way it looks, but also you know that he will be able to find his things more quickly and will be able to keep things neater. There has not been any yelling. Johnny is calm and so are you. And you have been his teacher. You have taught him through suggestions and hands-on experience. An added bonus is that you have been able to spend some quality time together and perhaps done some talking as you straightened things up.

So remember, you are the teacher, but in order to be able to teach effectively, you must be sure you instruct, not destruct.

***

Boundaries

Just think…if there were no marks on the road to define boundaries for us, we would just drive all over and probably get into an accident. Horns would be honking! Cars would be going in all different directions and traffic would be

4

impeded. Actually, without boundaries, it would take people longer to arrive at their destination and some would never arrive!

Just think…when there are no boundaries (margins) on writing paper, it is often hard to keep the letter or report neat. To the reader, the result may appear messy and not invite the reader to continue perusing the material. What you worked hard to compose would not even be read.

Just think…when you were a child and colored in your coloring books…if there were no lines to encompass the objects, your coloring would run all over and appear messy. With lines, the picture would be easy to see and you would find it easier to fill in the required spaces.

Just think…if there were no boundaries in a parking lot, you could park anywhere. If there were no boundaries around the school, you could walk anywhere and/or go anywhere when the bells would ring.

I guess by now, you get my drift. Boundaries define; they give direction. They help us know how and where to proceed. They help each day run more smoothly. Without boundaries, we are lost. We are like people in a forest without a compass. Our direction is unclear and we often go around in circles, frantically trying to find our way.

Similarly, if we, as parents, do not give our children boundaries, they, too, will lose their way. Sure, they may enjoy the freedom for a while, but in time they will get tired of and frustrated with getting lost. Disillusionment will set in; anger may ensue. They will continue searching in vain for light at the end of the tunnel.

The other day a young gal came into my office and told me that she hopes she can move back in with her father. I stared at her in disbelief. Just last year she had complained that living with Dad was hell.

"He has so many rules, Mrs. Cohen. I have a curfew. I have chores. I have time that he sets aside when I have to do my homework. I can't stand it!"

Well, she left Dad's and went to Mom's. And she thought she had gone to heaven. Mom was away a lot and really let Mary come and go as she pleased. But, in time, this freedom started catching up with Mary. Her grades started to plummet. Her life was no longer ordered and now she was admitting to me that she did miss that order. She missed having her life defined. Actually, she realized that she needed to have boundaries since they enabled her to accomplish so much more. They gave her direction.

5

So, folks, don't be afraid to have rules, to establish boundaries. Just make sure they are fair, appropriate and doable. Then, they will surely define the road your youngster should travel and make his destination that much easier to reach.

***

Stop, Look, and Listen

I still can hear my mother admonishing me to stop, look and listen before I crossed the street. What good advice, but it's also good to consider these three words when you actually do anything.

How many times do you stroll through the park, but really don't look at anything? You see things, sure, but do you really look at them? I went to the park during peak leaf time and this time brought my camera with me. What a difference it made! I really looked at the surroundings – at the bridges, ducks, children playing, fountains, and magnificent foliage. A matter of fact, I truly studied them since I wanted to capture great views on film. Each view took on an added significance and shined with beauty. Because I had my camera with me, my walk through the park was made more memorable…not only because I had recorded what I had seen on film, but also because I had recorded the sights in my mind. In truth, I had stopped and looked.

That takes me to another word…stop. How many of us stop during the day to just be…to let our minds wander, to perhaps take in the beauty around us, smell the fragrance of a flower, stop to see a child playing, stop to watch the snow fall, or just stop to do nothing…just relax and regroup. I venture to say that not many of us do stop during the day. We are so busy rushing from one thing to the next that we really don't savor what we have here and now. We don't give ourselves a chance to enjoy the moment. We don't give ourselves time to really work something out before we race on to the next thing.

A matter of fact, often when we are doing something, our minds are already racing, thinking about the next task or tasks we have to do. How unfortunate! How much is lost! It's sort of like eating a quick lunch, rather than sitting down and savoring it. Often times, we can't even remember what we had for lunch since we ate it so quickly and never gave thought to what we were doing. How many times have our children come in to tell us something, but they catch us as we're immersed in some task? We don't stop, but rather say, "Uh huh" at appropriate times and when they leave, we are left to wonder what had actually transpired. We never stopped to really listen.

And that takes me to the next word ...listen. Each day our youngsters stand in school as "The Pledge of Allegiance" is recited. But do they really listen as it is spoken? Do they really hear the words? How many would be able to recite the "Pledge" alone? How many truly understand its meaning? Why might they not? I suggest that the reason some don't comprehend what they are hearing is that they are not really listening; they have heard it said so many times that it has become like rote to them. What they hear are just words; what they do not hear is the meaning of each word.

Let's look at another example. Lucy keeps complaining about the same thing over and over again. You hear the words, but they have been repeated so often that you really don't stop to listen to them. Yet, it is important to really listen, to really hear what is being said, to really comprehend the meanings behind the words. In that way, you will be able to appropriately respond to what is being said.

Just think if all of us did stop, look, and listen...what a different world it would be. We would be so enriched by what we have stopped to see; we would be so much more in tune with our surroundings and the people with whom we have come in contact. Not only should we, as parents, be aware of these three words – stop, look, and listen – and incorporate them into our daily lives, but also we should teach our children to use them, too. They would comprehend better, not become so overwhelmed, and truly be able to embrace their years at school.

***

Are the Reins Too Tight?

Hey, I know it's not easy being a parent. I am a parent of three sons, so I have been there, done that, and am still doing it. Yes, there are parenting books, but no one can really tell you how to parent. You have to be there, be doing it, and your actions and thoughts depend upon the moment, the child, and the makeup of the family. What works for one child or for one parent will not necessarily work for another child or another parent. To tell you the truth, so much is trial and error and of course a little luck thrown in.

But I do feel that people can make suggestions, as long as the suggestions are well meaning and based on some sort of experience. If the suggestions work, feel free to wear them; if not discard them.

So, you guessed it, I have a suggestion. Reexamine the rein you have on your child. Is it appropriate or are you holding him too tightly? Then, again, are you not reining him in enough? What is right and how do you know that?

Let's look at Tim. He is given a lot of latitude. He virtually can come and go as he pleases. Mom and Dad are tied up with their own affairs, are never home, and Tim goes and does what he wants. How does this work? Not well, I am afraid. You see, Tim does not have any boundaries, and he needs them. Just think if there were no lines on the road, where would we all be driving? Yes, all over the place, and that's exactly where Tim is…he has no guidelines to define his actions. You might think this would make Tim happy. How wrong you are! Tim feels lost and confused. He questions his parents' interest in his daily pursuits. Do they really care? His path is not clearly marked, so he treads along it blindly. With Tim, the reins have to be made tighter.

Now, let's look at John. You keep him tightly reined. Afraid he will get into trouble, you have set a tight curfew that you strictly enforce, you wish to know his decisions at all times, and you expect him to check in with you when he is out. If he is having a friend come to the house, you expect him to ask your permission first. His room must me neat, his chores must be done, his grades must be good…. you get my drift.

Well, what happens? Actually there could be several scenarios. John can feel so uptight that he develops physical ailments…stomachaches, headaches, or whatever. He is able to achieve but at what price? Another option is that things are so insurmountable for him that he just caves in, decides he cannot possibly do anything, so he chooses to do nothing. Still another scenario might be that he decides to act out in school. Not able to voice opinions at home, unable to deviate at all from perfection, he chooses to misbehave in school. What's the message here? The reins are too tight. John needs some space. He is being choked and needs breathing room.

Now let's take a look at Kelly. She does have a curfew; however, if she finds she will be late, you expect a phone call. Scholastically, you expect her to do her best work, yet if she experiences difficulty you come to her aid and together you try to work it out. Yes, she has household chores, but they are not all consuming. Kelly still has time to socialize.

As for decision-making, you encourage her to make some of her own decisions. She does come to you for advice, but you want the decisions to be hers. That way she will own her choices and learn from them. Kelly will make mistakes. Her reins are not too tight and not too loose. She has room to move and sometimes she will move in the wrong direction, but at least she does have guidelines from you. How she chooses to use them is up to her. She does have some freedom of movement so she will make incorrect moves, but by doing so, she will grow, learn and become more confident in her ability to make appropriate choices.

So do give some thought to your reins. If they are too tight, they may choke your child; if they are too loose, he may fall through the cracks. But if they are somewhere in the middle, he will have the room to explore, to choose, and ultimately to mature.

***

Labeling

We live our lives by labels. Think about it. When we go into a market, we search the shelves for the labels we want. When we go into a department store, we look diligently for the clothes that have the label in them that fit us best. Our children will wear only a certain pair of jeans because it sports the right label. In addition to things having labels, people have them, too.

Many times children are labeled by classmates, teachers, or other family members. A mother nicknamed her child, "Spunky" because of his personality. Another parent, going through a difficult time in her life, named her child, "Hope." A group of students called a kid, "Shorty", but that kid had the last laugh because he grew to be 6 feet tall!

While labels can be helpful, they also can be harmful. Perhaps a child appears to be lazy since he takes so much time to complete his work. In reality, he has dyslexia that necessitates his working at a slower pace. Yet, teachers who may be unaware of this, begin to come down hard on the child and tell him to get busy and do his work more quickly. The teachers have labeled the child incorrectly and will cause the child to suffer unnecessarily.

Labeling may leave you, the parent, less able to see other components of your child's personality. You've pegged him a certain way, so you don't notice other qualities that he has. Try to avoid typecasting. Just because your son is good with his hands, don't only suggest to him that he should go into a field that is hands-on. This may hinder him from exploring different avenues. He may have other parts to him that haven't been nurtured and developed, yet once they are, he may find he has other talents that he wishes to pursue.

Labeling follows a child into adulthood. When you were younger, your friends thought you were shy and reserved. You internalized this and even now find it difficult to get up and give a speech. Their expectations have become your reality.

Next time you are in conversation with someone who knows your child, pay attention to the descriptive words he uses for your child. They may surprise you. What you think describes your child may not be your friend's description of him. Maybe at home, your son acts in a certain way to validate what you think of him; he knows what you expect, so he acts accordingly. But, maybe that is not the true image of your child. Have a talk with him. Discuss what he likes and dislikes. Ask him what he would like to do in the future. In other words, take time to reach beneath the surface. You may be surprised at what you will find.

Try to envision your child as multidimensional. I bet you will find many parts to him that make up the completed whole. Some of the parts are still being formed. Stay open to the person who is uniquely your child. By avoiding limiting your child with labels, you will be allowing him to be better able to explore his potential.

***

Mothers and Daughters

Wow…putting those two words together can be awesome or awful! Those of you who are daughters and/or mothers will get my drift, I'm sure. I know during this past school year, I have heard so many mother and daughter stories that are filled with anger, dismay, confusion, and hurt. Just why is this? Well, I have given it some thought and will attempt to give you some answers. If they work for you and you see yourself, that's great. If they are not appropriate, then don't buy into them. I am talking about the difficulties, not the pleasures that a mother/daughter relationship involves, because being a daughter, I know there are also many pleasures.

Just today Susie came into my office. Her grades had been slipping, she had been cutting classes, her boyfriend had broken up with her and she had been having issues with her mother.

"Why is she always in my face, Mrs. Cohen? Why does she find fault with everything I do? Why can't she trust me? Am I that bad?"

She also told me that her mom yells and screams at her, and wants to know where she is at all times. Unfortunately, Susie was losing her cool with her mom and instead of listening quietly to what her mother has to say, she would get all wound up, start to yell, and then of course, everything would escalate.

From listening to her, it was apparent that Susie was not always right either. She had acted out, but not to the point of mother's reprisals. So together we looked at the issues and after some discussion, we both were able to glean some insight. Mom had gotten into some trouble when she was a teenager. So, instead of looking at her daughter as her daughter, she was looking at her daughter as an extension of herself. As she looked at her, she would displace her mistakes and place them on her daughter. Therefore, she was afraid that her daughter would make or had already made the same mistakes that she, the mother, had made. Sounds confusing, but it happens so often. Perhaps Mom wasn't trusted as a young girl, so now she doesn't trust her daughter, or perhaps Mom was trusted as a young girl and did get away with a lot of things behind her mother's back. Perhaps she is afraid that if she trusts Susie, then Susie will be doing inappropriate things.

Sometimes, too, moms are jealous of their daughters. I know that sounds harsh, but sometimes it is true. Mom is getting older; her daughter looks young and vibrant. Maybe the daughter is enjoying things that Mom never could enjoy when she was younger. Perhaps Mom is gaining weight and her daughter has a beautiful figure. Mom gets resentful and maybe she dislikes herself for getting resentful, but she still takes her resentment out by yelling at her daughter.

Another scenario could be that things are not going well at home. Mom and Dad are not getting along. Mom is really angry with herself for many of the issues. Mom doesn't take out her frustrations on Dad, nor is she able to take them out on herself, so she takes her anger out on her daughter whom she sees as a continuation of herself.

You know, Moms, when you look in the mirror, the image you see is yours. Yet, remember, when you look at your daughter, you are seeing a different image, an image of your daughter, a person with her own actions, responses, abilities, desires, and attitude.

And you, daughters, hang up your anger and resentment. Is Mom acting out because of a hidden agenda? Look at your mom as a real person with issues of her own. Recognizing these things will make a difference.

***

11

Contracts

A contract is an agreement between two parties or more with parameters decided upon by the involved parties. We usually think of contracts when they are used in law and business; however, they are also used by schools and families and serve a wonderfully useful purpose.

Agreement is the key word. If you agree to something and I agree to something, then it has a better chance of working. Ponder the following. Mom comes into my office. Her son is doing very poorly in school. Groundings have been meted out, but to no avail. Mom and Dad are clearly at their wits end! What to do? All they want is a little peace and tranquility. I call the young man into my office without his parents. I figure he will probably talk more freely to me alone, and I have already heard his parents' side of the story. Through discussion, I find that he's very upset with his parents. Why am I not surprised? He feels some of the household demands made on him are unfair.

When I ask him if he has spoken to his parents and shared those feelings, he looks up at me and responds, "Nah…what good would it do…they never listen to me anyway. They have their own agenda. Mine doesn't cut it with them and they start yelling right away. Then, before I know it, I'm yelling, too, and nothing gets accomplished."

After more discussion, we both come to the conclusion that Joe is getting bad grades to get back at his folks. We examine this logic and find some holes.

"I mean, whom are you really hurting, Joe?" I ask.

Thinking it over, he realizes he is hurting himself, but he hopes he is hurting his parents, too, since they deserve to be hurt. After all, they are upsetting him, so why shouldn't he upset them?

"Ah", I continue, "but at what consequence?"

Joe is angry with his folks; his folks are angry with him. Clearly, there is turmoil and frustration. In order to vent these emotions so they can be dealt with, I decided that Joe and his folks should be in my office together since my place is kind of neutral and non-threatening. Perhaps, as a facilitator, I can get everyone to air his or her concerns in a calm fashion.

When they all enter my office, it is interesting to see how they place themselves in the chairs. Mom and Dad sit very close to each other on one side of the room and Joe takes his chair and moves it away from his parents to the other side of the room. I can easily read beneath the body language and sense their discomfort with each other. I give each one time to speak without the other interrupting. That is essential! Interruptions make one lose one's train of thought and sort of diminish what one is saying. After each has aired his issues, I look at each one and tell him that I think I have a plan. I talk to them about writing a contract…nothing fancy, nothing that you have to have a doctorate to write, just a simple contract stating five things that they would each like to have happen. Each would be committed to make changes. Moreover, each would become aware of his responsibilities. An important plus would be that Joe would think that his parents care enough to listen to his wants, too, and to incorporate them into the contract. The contract would become a written compromise.

Discussion ensued and both parents and Joe leave promising to draft the contract and get back to me. They all feel empowered. Now they have a plan to help them rectify an unpleasant situation.

The next morning, the phone rings. Dad calls to tell me that they had sat down around the kitchen table and discussed each major point that was written down to determine if the point were viable, if it could be followed, if it were fair and if it were workable. He couldn't believe how much they all had communicated. Finally, the contract was written according to each one's needs.

About a week passes. I call Joe in and ask how it's going. He tells me that the contract is posted on the refrigerator. If Joe wants to do something and Dad is quick to respond, "No," Joe has only to point to the terms of the contract. Arguments are precluded from happening. In similar fashion, when the son balks at something, Mom and Dad turn to the contract and the negative discussion is ended. I tell them to review the contract after two weeks. Changes can be made if necessary and agreed upon by both parties.

***

Is the Road Too Wide?

Parents were called on the phone. Ben wasn't doing well in school, numerous conferences had been held, the vice-principal had become involved, teachers were writing him up, progress reports were being issued; yet nothing constructive had occurred. Inappropriate behavior continued to ensue. Ben would sleep in class, not do the prepared assignments, be tardy or even skip school. His grades were at an all time low. When punishments were issued for the infractions, he would choose not to do them. Clearly, my interventions were not working. Something had to be done. Someone had to change and I didn't think it had to be me!

His mother was reached and came immediately to school. Sitting across from me in my office, Mom looked very agitated. Wringing her hands, she told me that she just didn't know what to do with Ben anymore. She talks to him, she threatens him with punishments, she reasons with him, but to no avail.

And then, as I listened and looked at her, I saw her crumple in front of me and burst into tears. I waited for a moment, handed her the requisite tissue, and then gently asked her what punishments had been meted out. As she spoke to me, I realized that none had been enacted; they had merely been talked about. So, in essence, a lot of screaming had taken place, but nothing concrete had been done.

With further conversation, I was able to surmise that Mom and Dad never really followed through on their threats. It seemed that one parent would be the good cop and one would be the bad cop and Ben knew just how to play each one. A master at manipulation, he would make all kinds of promises to improve, his parents would give in, and Ben would start his downward spiral again. I told Mom that the road was too wide.

"Excuse me," she interjected, looking a little dumbfounded. "The road is what? What does that have to do with my son?"

I hastened to explain. "When the road is very wide, it gives you a lot of room to do different things as you drive. If allowed, you can make a u-turn; you can move from lane to lane. You don't have tight, tight boundaries. You can move a little bit more at will."

Continuing this train of thought, I said, "Now, let's take a look at the narrow country road. You have to stay in your lane. You have narrow boundaries and must adhere to them. We can compare this to boundaries that you make for your child. If they are undefined, your child will venture all over the place. If they are too wide, he still may not know which way to go and will go off in different directions; but if they are narrow, he will have no alternatives. He will know what route he has to travel in order to arrive at his destination."

Ben's mom looked at me and said, "My husband and I really have not made any firm boundaries for Ben. I guess we thought we were being kind to him by not doing anything. We didn't mean any harm."

Shaking my head in acquiescence, I said, "I know. I'm sure you did think you were doing the right thing. But Ben does need guidelines to help him stay on the right track. In addition, he needs to hear the same ones from you and your husband; otherwise, he will be confused."

***

Overbearing or Just Plain Caring

I gotta tell you, the distinction between overbearing and caring is a slim one, but so important to consider. As parents, counselors, teachers, and friends, we all truly care about each other. We want to reach out and help. But in trying to reach out and help, are we being overbearing? Are we smothering the person?

Let's look at two examples. Jen comes home. Her report card is not the best. You get in her face, really question her about her grades and push her to tell you what's troubling her. You may get answers; you may not. Then, you decide to call the guidance counselor and put Jen on progress reports. In addition, you ground her from using the telephone at night so that she will think about her poor grades and work hard to improve them. Okay, so you have done all that, but have you really looked at what you've done? You were the one who called the counselor, you were the one who put her on progress reports, and you were the one who grounded Jen.

Now, step back for a minute. Have you given Jen space to try to work something out for herself? Have you given her choices? Yes, you have been caring, caring enough to tell her what to do, but in so doing, you have been overbearing. You have smothered Jen with your good intentions and have not allowed her to fend for herself and then to see if her fending for herself will enable her to improve. She may fail again and that's all right. Everyone has permission to fail and sometimes only when a person falls down will that person reassess the situation and then be able to change and work hard to pick herself up.

Now let's look at Tom. Naturally, you want to be part of his life. So, when Tom comes home, you ask him how things are going. He kind of grunts in reply to your query. You get incensed with his lack of response and proceed to ask him more questions. He stares at you with a vacant look on his face and may say, "I dunno"…or just shrug his shoulders. The point is you are not getting the answers you want. Actually, Tom probably wants to just be left alone. But you sense that he is unhappy so you probe even further and you know what, Tom retreats even further!!!

Finally, he may look at you and snarl, "Just get out of my face" and with that he slams the door and hides out in his safety zone, his room. You are left standing there feeling horrible. I mean what did you do to deserve this kind of treatment? After all, you were just trying to help. You feel hurt, you feel used, and you feel shut out. But in Tom's mind, you have been overbearing and he just wants to be left alone!

Okay, so what's the answer? You care and you want your child to know you care and I think that's great. But as you reach out and care, do watch your child's responses. Is he trying to ignore you? Is he accepting your suggestions? Does he feel uncomfortable? Be aware of these signs and adjust your caring accordingly. Even though you may wish to reach out, stop yourself if your child is not being receptive. Do say that you're interested and you are there to help, but you will only help if your child wishes it.

Actually, if you do make all the suggestions for your child, you are not allowing him the space to explore and to figure things out for himself. You are not allowing him to take ownership of his actions. You are not allowing him to grow, to mature, and to eventually stand on his own two feet. Breathing space is necessary, so reassess your actions and do give him some room.

***

What's In It For You?

You know we all like to reach out and touch someone. We like to help someone. We like to listen, to give advice and just be there, but have we ever examined why we like to do those things?

Many times it is because the other person needs assistance and we are being a good person. But sometimes, there could be a hidden ulterior motive. Maybe we really need to reach out to satisfy our own wants. Perhaps we never felt worthwhile. By reaching out to others we become validated, we become important, we become necessary. We buy them many gifts; we had never received too many. We give a compliment because maybe we are fishing to get one in return.

Perhaps we were lousy students in high school. By pushing our child to really excel, we, in turn, are getting a second chance to excel. Yes, we do care about him, but inwardly there is another reason we are helping him.

Maybe we encourage our son to play a sport. Perhaps he really doesn't want to, but he doesn't want to upset us so he goes along with our wishes. We yell and scream from the sidelines. We are filled with pride, but there's another reason for our feelings. When we were young, we rode pine, we sat on the bench, but now, through our son, we have a second chance.

Our son wants to apply to a certain college; we want him to apply to a different one. Is it because we never had a chance to apply to that one or maybe we were rejected when we did apply?

Our daughter brings home a date. We really don't like him, yet he has wonderful qualities. Perhaps it's because we remember some negative experiences we had concerning the dating scene and don't want the same thing to happen to our daughter.

And what about smothering our kid? That does happen. We so want to get love. Our parents didn't pay attention to us, so we overburden our child with all the love and attention we can bestow. Yet, what's in it for us? I'll tell you…love that we didn't get before; love that we desperately need now.

You know all our actions are really reactions to bits and pieces that are inside of us…the wants, the desires, and the past experiences that have molded us. And that's okay. What's not okay is to not recognize why we are doing something, to not recognize the other person's wants and desires. Are we meeting those or are we meeting ours? Are we really doing what our child needs and wants, or are we doing what we need and want?

The other day a young lady came into my office. She poignantly said, "You know what really bugs me, Mrs. Cohen? My dad…he's always on my case to be so good at my sport. He yells, he screams, he carries on when I make a mistake, and you know what my grandma told me…he really stunk at the same sport!! So why is he doing this to me?"

I went on to explain to her that it wasn't because he was mean or mercilessly pushing her to excel; rather, it was filling a void in his life. It was a chance for him to succeed through her.

I know we all want to do what's best for our children, but making them in an image that we want, that makes us feel better, is not the answer. So do question yourself and ask "What's in it for me?" and then regroup and do something that will answer, "What's in it for them?"

***

Are You Living Through Your Child?

You know, it is so hard as a parent not to live through your child. It is so hard not to encourage your child to become all that you wish him to be. It is so hard not to be upset when you see your child making the same mistakes that you made as a child. It is so difficult to see your weaknesses in your child. Or perhaps it is so difficult for you to recognize the fact that your child does not have your weaknesses or perhaps does not have your strengths.

But whoa…I mean settle down…your child is your child, but alas your child is a unique human being. Although he may resemble you physically, he does not totally resemble you. I still do a slow burn when I see a dad yelling and screaming as he watches his child at a sporting event. I am sure the kid is cringing. He gets up to bat. He whiffs. The dad yells at him, telling him not to kill the ball, to address the ball, to swing straight through. Clearly, he is agitated. The boy swings and whiffs again. The father stamps his foot in disgust. Now the boy has two strikes. There are three men on base. Will the son be the hero or the goat? The pitch comes in. The son watches the ball, but he seems unable to swing. He looks at the ball as it whizzes by and the ump calls the third strike. Dejectedly, the boy flings the bat behind him, and with head hanging low, walks back to the dug out. Dad emits some expletives and clearly is an unhappy parent. It seems in his day he was a leading hitter for his high school team. Why can't Eric excel as he did?

Did Dad ever stop to think that perhaps Eric does not really want to play ball, perhaps he is only doing it to please Dad? Actually, he would rather participate in another sport or maybe join an after school club, but he doesn't want to disappoint his dad. But here's the rub…the more he wants to please Dad, the more he messes up. He just can't take the pressure. If only Dad would back down. Maybe if Dad would not come to the game, Eric would find that he is able to hit better and may in fact begin to really enjoy playing ball. With enjoyment may even come increased prowess.

This scenario could be repeated with other activities, hobbies, and schoolwork. It is so important for parents to realize that each child is unique with his own capabilities and these capabilities are what make each child special. Instead of pushing your child to do something, take time to really listen to what your child wants to do. After all, it is your child's life and you should not try to be living it for him or try having him live it for you. Revel in your child's strengths, rejoice in them, encourage them, and they will become even stronger. Recognize your child's weaknesses. Help him to cope with them and to understand that it is okay to have weaknesses. After all, no one is perfect.

I remember talking to a quilter who told me that each time she makes a quilt she has to include a flaw. I looked at her and said, "But why? Don't you want the quilt to be the best that you can possibly create?"

She looked at me, shook her head, and said, "No, I want the quilt to have an imperfection, to show the world that it was made by a human being and humans are not perfect. Only a supreme being has perfection."

What a wise lady. If only we could all live by her words and realize it's okay not to excel in everything. If only we could stop to realize that each person does excel in his own way. If only we could realize that we cannot and should not live through our children. After all, they have their own areas in which they excel.

So, parents, do look outside of yourselves and realize how uniquely beautiful your children are and how much they have to offer. It may not be what you have to offer, and that's okay. Remember, it's what they have to offer that you should recognize and encourage.

***

Whose Story Is It?

You know, how many times have you said to your son or your daughter, "Hey, what's the problem? Tell me your story; let me hear what's troubling you?"

And then, perhaps he does decide to share, but here's the rub. As he tells you his story, you start interjecting with stories of your own, so instead of really listening to his events, you start sharing yours. A matter of fact, your mind is racing ahead to ideas of your own that you wish to bring to the table so that you really are not zeroing in on what your child is trying to impart to you.

And you know what? Your child feels this, internalizes it, and then says to himself, "Why should I bother telling my story? Obviously it's not that important and is not really being listened to."

So, you guessed it, your child shuts up and decides not to continue with his tale. I mean what's in it for him? Nothing...so why bother? A matter of fact, it is hurtful and annoying to him that you are not really listening; he does not feel worthwhile. You, on the other hand, are busy with your own agenda; you're caught up with it and therefore miss much of the gist of what your child has been trying to tell you. Sound familiar? It probably does if you really stop to think about it.

That's because the hardest thing is to really listen. We are so busy thinking ahead and wanting to get our own two cents in that we do not give the other person space to speak. We may hear for the moment, but we do not listen for a length of time.

I remember one mother who came into my office. She said to her son, "Tell me why you are so angry at me. If you just share your feelings with me, then we can deal with them together."

I thought, "Boy, this is pretty good."

Well, her son started to open his mouth, but as soon as he did, the mother quickly interrupted and raced ahead with her own thoughts, not allowing her child time to get a word in edgewise.

It was actually incredible and then she had the audacity to say, "See, you really never let me know how you feel; so what do you expect from me anyway… I am not a mind reader, you know."

And so the conversation progressed…although it was clearly a one sided conversation which left neither party too thrilled!

Next time you ask your child to share, make sure you button your lip; make sure you sit with your child, have eye contact, show your child you are truly interested in what he is saying, and listen, listen, listen. Do not interrupt until your child is done imparting his tale. Then, do feel free to offer your thoughts, but offer them without negating what he shared with you. Make him feel that his thoughts are important and you do that by paying attention to him. You'll be surprised; you will learn so much and will actually encourage your child to share more information with you.

Remember, it is important to keep in mind just whose story it is.

***

18 Years…So Few, But So Important

It never ceases to amaze me how much the first 18 years affect someone's life. Think about it…if you muse back to elementary school, I am sure you can still conjure up images of happenings on the playground and faces of favorite teachers and friends. If you were bullied, or made fun of in any fashion, that, too, left an indelible mark. I still remember going to my 20th high school reunion.

Lisa approached me and asked my forgiveness.

For what, I wondered and she responded, "You know, in 7th grade, I was really mad at you and I pulled down your crinoline as you walked up to the front of the class."(I'm dating myself…that's a slip!)

Well, I hated to disappoint Lisa, but I had no recollection of the happening. Obviously, she, the perpetrator, had been haunted by it for years!

Students will come into my office and tell me how afraid they are of speaking in front of the class. Through further conversation, I often find that when they were younger, kids snickered at them as they rose to speak.

I can still remember the anorexic young girl to whom I spoke. She was a senior and fading away before my eyes. It seems in elementary school and junior high school, she was always made fun of because of her weight. Determined never to be the butt of jokes again, she decided to lose weight by not eating.

I look at some of the "popular" kids at school and the athletes who seem to have a certain swagger as they walk. These kids walk down the hallways with their shoulders squared and their heads held high. I know that many will continue to walk through life that way because of the foundation that their first eighteen years has provided.

Then, I look at the kids who walk with their heads down, who sort of shuffle along and don't acknowledge people to the right or the left. Either they are the unhappy campers or they are just painfully shy. Will their demeanor change as they mature?

I think about the young lady who came into my office and told me that she loved English! Her eyes were beaming, her face was flushed with excitement, and her mouth was going a mile a minute as she told me that she wished to be an English teacher. You see, her current English teacher had really turned her on to learning English, to seeing beyond the words on the page, to putting her thoughts on paper in a meaningful fashion, and to making deceased authors come to life through their writings. A course in school has made a difference to this young lady and will definitely impact the rest of her life through the vocation she chooses and probably in the way she, too, presents English to her eventual students.

By now, I am sure I have proven my point. The halls of learning do impact a young person's life. Just 1/5 of their lives are spent in grades K-12, yet those years often define and determine the next 4/5ths!!!

As a parent, notice your child. Really see him. Is he very quiet? What does he say about school? Does the phone ring for him? How are his grades? Who are his friends? Are you listening to his wants and needs and steering him towards those things in which he can excel…or are you so tired when you come home that your eyes are unseeing and your ears are unhearing?

Yes, 18 years is a short time in your child's life, but the impact is a long one. Make the impact be fruitful, make it be positive, make it allow your child to become more self-assured and more ready to grapple with the next 4/5th of his life in a fulfilling and self-actualizing manner.

***

Parenting or Pestering

This morning I was thinking about these two words and how inextricably they are intertwined. I don't think one word can really exist without the other.

In order to parent effectively, it is important to "stay on" your children. You must be aware of what they are doing, not be afraid to ask questions, and be able and willing to establish some rules. In a way, this intrusion can be called pestering, but I would rather euphemistically call it parenting.

Just the other day, a parent called me on the phone to discuss his son's progress or lack thereof. He just couldn't understand why his child was doing so badly.

He said, "You know, we give him everything; there's food on the table at night, he has all the clothes he needs and we even pay for the insurance on the car. He has a great room where he can study and a state-of-the-art computer. What possibly could be the problem?"

"Well," I explained, "it is apparent that he does have some wonderful tangible things, but what about the intangible ones? Do you set times when he should be doing homework? Do you check to see that it is done? Do you give him a curfew so he does not feel free to stay out till all hours? Do you tell him what is expected of him in school and help him achieve this? Do you listen to him when he comes home from school and help him sort out his problems? In other words, Mr. Jones, are you a true presence in his life…are you in his face just a little bit?"

Mr. Jones thought for a moment. I could almost hear him hemming and hawing. Finally, he retorted, "No… I wouldn't want to be accused of pestering him."

"Ah, Mr. Jones, but that's where I believe you are wrong. In order to really parent, you need to pester. You need to make certain that things are occurring. You need to give direction. A matter of fact, if truth be told, your son really wants you to pester him."

You know, kids like to act as if they are all grown up, as if they know everything and we as parents know nothing. Recently I was giving my eldest son some directives. He is a lawyer and has a wonderful young family.

After I spoke, he looked at me and asked, "How old am I?"

Not skipping a beat, I said, " I know how old you are, but you are and will always be my son. And when I stop pestering, it means I have stopped caring."

So, my readers, don't be afraid to pester. Just be certain that what you pester about is meaningful, appropriate, and doable. Children need some pestering since they need direction, they need motivation, they need encouragement, and they need your interference. Yes, they need your parenting and pestering is part of the parenting package!

***

Parents, Kids, Coaches, Sports

Wow! Even though the above title has just four words, it is power packed and today more than ever, those four components are being looked at, digested, and questioned.

As a mother of three sons who each lettered in three sports and garnered accolades, believe me I have been there. I have rejoiced in their successes and despaired over their failures. Their days of glory buoyed my spirits; their days of defeat allowed gloom and doom to overcome me. Yes, I lived vicariously through them. What parent hasn't? At times, I wished to take away their hurt; at times I wished to take exception with the coaches, or the refs and umpires who…I was certain…miscalled some important plays. And what parent hasn't felt like that, too? I enjoyed the camaraderie of other parents as I sat at the edge of my seat watching a game. We yelled together, we cheered, we felt as if we were out there playing the game. So, yes, I do know where a sports parent comes from.

But, I must admit, that I still do not understand the extreme emotions and actions that envelop certain parents. By yelling and screaming incessantly at the umpires and refs, by lowering ourselves and calling them certain names, by blaming them constantly for our sons' and daughters' receiving a T, aren't we missing something? Aren't we maybe missing where the problem really lies? Are we looking at our children through rose-colored glasses? Isn't it possible that our children could deserve the T, the strike, or whatever? Or, perhaps, they do not deserve the call; yet, isn't it possible that the ref or ump could have made a mistake just because he or she is human?

As parents, and I know this is hard, we must keep things in perspective. We must remember, too, that we are the ones to whom our children look for guidance and support. We are the ones whom they will strive to emulate, yet what image are we presenting when we yell, scream, blame others, or even fight? Are we not giving our children license to act in the same manner?

It is good to get involved, it is good to care, but let's remember to care appropriately. Let's remember to praise when praise is warranted, and to give constructive criticism when that is warranted. I know it's frustrating to see your child "ride pine", to languish on the bench, but instead of complaining, seek out the coach and ask why. Have your child talk to him. Remember, at the high school level, the coach is looking to win and in order to do so s/he has to utilize the best players. How can yours become one of the best? Let your child strive to do that with practice and encouragement. If your child cannot stand the competition, then perhaps sports are not for him. That's okay. There are other avenues of involvement.

Ask yourself, is your child playing sports because he wants to or is he playing sports to please you? Are you always in his face after a game asking him why he did not do such and such, or do you try to assess his playing in a non-threatening and constructive manner? I still remember my sons telling my husband and me that they so enjoyed their involvement in sports because my husband knew nothing about sports. He had no idea when the ball was dribbled well, when the pass was well executed, or when the ball was hit in the most effective manner. So, he smiled, gave encouragement, and watched every play. Groans could be heard around him, but not from him. After each game, he always congratulated our sons. After all, they tried; they did their best. Yet, he did commiserate, too.

I remember my middle son telling me after a really tough football loss that losing hurts more than winning feels good. So, we listened, we didn't try to talk him out of this feeling, we allowed him to feel it, to look at his plays as objectively as possible, and then to suck it up and go on. We tried not to castigate, not to point fingers, but rather just to be there to listen.

Don't get me wrong. I, who have played sports, was not always as laid back as my husband. I even ran onto the football field once after my quarterback son was sacked! But I learned. I could not do for my sons. They had to learn to do for themselves. They had to learn to take responsibilities for their actions, and they could not learn that if the sole responsibility and blame were placed on the coaches, refs, umpires, or other team members. Tolerance and understanding came with the more games that we attended. We learned to count to 10.

You know, the playing field of life is just like the playing field for sports. There, too, children are team players; they have to work together, take responsibility for their actions, look at themselves with their eyes wide open, and work diligently in order to succeed.

Then, too, you, as parents, have to respond on the field of life in the same manner you would on the field of sports. Support your children, be there for them, be realistic about their pursuits, give constructive criticism, be there for their failures, be there for their successes, and encourage them to take ownership of their actions, teaching them that blaming is counter productive. On whichever field you are playing or watching, how you act will definitely make a difference.

***

Walk Barefoot and Feel the Pebbles

I was listening to a lecture the other day and I heard the speaker talk about walking barefoot. Immediately, my ears perked up since the comment seemed so strange to me. Yet, as he continued, the words started to ring true and lasted with me my whole drive home.

Think about the following for a moment. When you are walking outside with shoes on, what do you feel? Actually, the shoes protect you from the heat, or from the cold, or even from sharp objects that may be lying around. But, by protecting you, they stop you from feeling, from connecting with your surroundings, from learning to deal with them.

Now take this a step further. By not feeling what's underfoot, do you really know what's going on? And of course, that brings me to the point of this article – by protecting yourself, you are often hampering yourself. You are precluding yourself from really feeling the essence of things, from really getting a sense of what is occurring. How much better it is to feel some pain, to know what is occurring, than to walk on a seemingly smooth surface that really is not smooth at all. The pain makes you pause, think, and check out the situation. The smooth walk allows you to just continue walking without noticing anything underfoot.

How many times do we decide to put our shoes on, to keep ourselves out of the "dirty" parts of life? How much easier it is to keep our feet clean, rather than getting them dirty. After all, when they become dirty, there is cleaning up to do.

Ah…but isn't that what should happen in life? Shouldn't we allow ourselves to become dirty, to immerse ourselves in our surroundings, to really feel what is underfoot? Then, we can examine the situation, and start to make appropriate plans to clean it up.

As parents we naturally wish to protect our children. We want to make sure they are wearing their shoes. Yet, in doing this, are we really helping them? No. Instead, we are protecting them from seeing and feeling the good as well as the bad. We are giving them a false view of life, so that when they finally do see it and consequently feel it, they will not know how to deal with it. It's all right for them to witness pain; it's all right for them to know about poverty. It's all right for them to know that they don't always have to make a team or if they do make the team that they don't always have to start. It's all right for them to get a C. It's all right for them to feel hurt when someone has hurt their feelings. It's all right for them to feel your anger when they have upset you. It's all right for them to realize they cannot have a car unless they work hard to earn money for it. It's all right for them to hear the word no. It's all right for them to fall when they try to skate. In time, they will learn to glide smoothly.

Yes, life is imperfect, so do let them exhibit and feel those imperfections; let them feel the pebbles.

***

Decisions

The other day I had a meeting with parents and their son. As we sat in my office, I started to ask some questions. Each time I would ask a question, Mom or Dad would answer it. That was okay, if I were always asking the question to Mom and Dad. But you see, that wasn't always the case. Sometimes I was asking Brian how he was doing, how he was feeling…in essence, what was happening. And each time, Mom and Dad would answer for him. The kid clearly did not have laryngitis or a hearing issue. It was obvious that he could hear me, yet it was also obvious that Mom and Dad did all the talking for him.

I have to tell you I have seen that scenario over and over and it is a most telling phenomenon. It doesn't tell me that Mom and Dad are bad parents; rather they are good parents and think that they are acting in a correct manner. What it does tell me is that they are the ones who are the decision-makers. They are the ones who do the thinking for Brian. They are the ones who tell him what should be done, when it should be done, and how it should be done. Brian is like a marionette…the parents pull the strings and he reacts. Why does this happen?

Well, think about it. Since he was born, Mom and Dad have been making all Brian's decisions. When he was a baby, they had to figure out what he wanted when he cried, what he was trying to say when he started to speak, and give him direction when he started to venture forth. After all, he is their child and a child cannot possibly know what a parent knows. They didn't want him to fall down, so instead they felt if they told him how to do things, if they made decisions for him, he would not get hurt. It seemed to be working, so they continued to use the same modus operandi. I mean if it isn't broken, don't fix it. Right? Nah…wrong!

What they lost sight of was that Brian was growing up. Yes, he had listened to what they told him, he had internalized a lot of it, and now he should be able to walk alone. They could still be there to guide, but he must be allowed to walk by himself. If he is not allowed to walk alone, he will never do it. He needs to make decisions on his own. He needs to be allowed to fall flat on his face; if not, he will never have to learn how to pick himself up. He will never learn the coping skills that are so important in order to be successful in the world.

You know, decisions are involved in all of life. From the simplest things from getting up in the morning, to what to eat, to the more difficult decision of what college to attend, decisions must be made every day. And the weird thing is, only from making the wrong decisions, can we learn what the right decisions should be.

In addition, when Brian is allowed to make decisions, to think for himself, he will take ownership for his decisions. If they don't work, it is his problem. He chose the decision. And if it does work, he will feel empowered and good about himself.

As parents, it is so hard to sit back and allow your child to make decisions. You so want him to make the right ones, but what message are you giving him if you do not allow him to make any decisions? Perhaps he is getting the message that you do not trust his judgment; perhaps he getting the message that you don't think he is mature enough or smart enough to do things on his own; perhaps he is getting the message that he cannot make decisions, so he should not even try to do so without a parent's advice. And you know what…this last thought is stultifying. It will incapacitate your child; it will stop him from growing, from standing up on his own two feet.

So, you parents out there- step back from the decision- making process. But not entirely. Certainly present what you think and what you want and why you think such and such is a good idea, but then leave the actual decision making to your child. He's in high school; he is growing up. Do allow him to do that.

***

Roots and Wings

So many times we hear how important it is to give your children roots and wings. Yet, what exactly does the expression mean? And when we understand the true meaning, how can we practice it?

When your children are born, their slates are clean. Yes, they may have certain genetic traits, but for the most part, they are lumps of clay waiting to be molded. Through parenting, through our discussions, suggestions and actions, our children grow, adapt to their surroundings and develop personalities. Indeed, we try to give them roots; we try to enable them to understand appropriate ways to behave; we instill our ethics. We give them a basic understanding of who we are and who they are. By doing this, we are giving them a firm foundation; we are giving them roots.

But, here's the problem. Now that they have the roots, now that they are maturing, when do we step back and give them wings? When do we allow them to take flight, to deal with their surroundings, to make decisions and to just learn to be without our constant assistance?

Let's take a look at Jenny. Mom has always made all Jenny's decisions. Jenny has not really been given choices and asked to choose between **two** things; instead she has been given the **one** thing. Now it's time for colleges…a big decision making time. All of a sudden, Jenny's grades begin to plummet. Other kids are bringing me their applications; Jenny has not brought me one. I call her in. She tells me that she thinks she wants to take a year off; she doesn't want to go to college right away. Of course, I look at her grades and subsequent warnings and tell her that at this rate, she won't have to worry about college.

Then, the light bulb goes on and I think, that's it, she doesn't want to worry about college; she doesn't want to have to make a decision. In fact, she doesn't know how to make a decision, since she hasn't been allowed to gain expertise in that area. Perhaps, I quietly suggest, that's why her grades have plummeted. Perhaps, with low grades, she will not have to make the decision about leaving home and going to college. After all, leaving home and having to make decisions must really be scary thoughts for Jen.

I had a long talk with Mom. Not surprisingly, Mom thought she was doing the right thing for Jen. By making all the decisions, Mom really believed that life would be easier for Jen and that Jen would not be apt to make many mistakes.

But children need to be given wings; they need to start making decisions at an early age. For instance, when they go into a market, you can ask them if they want the Oreos or the chocolate chips. You might ask if they want to invite Carol or Sally, but not both, over to the house after school. By starting out with making small decisions, children will become more skillful in making larger decisions. They will be given the space to grow, to take flight. Oh, but then what about the mistakes? They **need** to make the mistakes. Only through making mistakes will they learn.

When your children are born, nurture them, give them roots, make their decisions, but as they start to venture forth to school, as they start to really comprehend the world around them, do include them in decision making. Do give them permission to grow wings and take flight. If the roots are firm, they will not fly away forever; they will use their wings to explore, but they will continue to revisit their roots, too. Yes, roots and wings, both are essential in helping children develop to their fullest.

***

The Invisible Boy

Yes, you are existing, you know you are existing. You can see yourself in the mirror. You need food, and water. You need sleep. You can walk, you can talk, but yet, you don't feel that people can see you. How can that be? You can see yourself, so why can't others? What's the deal?

Believe it or not, this feeling is shared by so many, yet not really discussed that often. The other day Tim came into my office. His grades have been very low, but his aptitude is high.

"Tim, I just looked at this term's grades. They are not good, yet when I looked at your test scores I noticed that you are very bright. What seems to be the trouble? How is everything going? Something has to be going on."

Tim looked at me, thought for just a split second and then emitted tersely, "No, nothing."

Well, I am not one to give up easily. Clearly he was a guy who was hurting big time, so making sure the door to my office was closed, I decided to just sit there, look at him and let silence fill the air. He fidgeted, I fidgeted…after all, silence does do that. It's uncomfortable, and that's the mood I wanted. I wanted Tim to feel uncomfortable, to feel he had to say something in order to lift the oppressive prevailing mood.

"Mrs. Cohen, you're right. There are some issues at home. I don't know how to really explain them, but I guess I just kind of feel invisible."

Tim went on to tell me that he really does not feel like anyone notices him. He walks through the hallways and no one acknowledges him. He goes home to a house that is filled with turmoil and everyone is so busy mired in his own muck that Tim is not noticed and when he does ask a question, he is shunned, or told summarily, "Keep still, I'm busy" or "This does not concern you." Therefore, he often chooses to hole up in his room and to keep his opinions and comments to himself.

He is there, but not there. He chooses not to be seen, not to cause trouble. He doesn't want to be yelled at, and he would rather be ignored. It is easier. In time, he decides to shut down his feelings; if he allows himself to feel, it hurts too much that he is not noticed. Yes it's better not to feel, to just be, but is he really "being"? He does get angry, but keeps the anger inside. Because of this, the anger turns to depression. He has trouble sleeping and eating. Every day seems like an eternity. Everyday seems joyless. He has no energy. He cannot get out of bed. All his energy is being used up in a negative way.

Interestingly, though, Tim decides to pierce his ear and his eyebrow. He decides to wear "outlandish clothes" and to dye his hair a multitude of colors. Why? I think it's because he wants desperately to have some sense of identity, to feel that he does exist, to say to the world, "Now you have to recognize me!" He cannot do it with words; words get him into trouble; instead he does it with his outward trappings.

I call Mom and Dad into my office. We discuss the way Tim is feeling. Because they are so embroiled in their own misery they have not stopped to notice how he is feeling. Actually, they don't notice Tim at all! In truth, he has become invisible to them. They are shocked with our discussion. They had no idea how Tim was feeling. How would they? They never took time to ask, to listen, or to notice. They were glad he disappeared into his room. That was one less issue they had to deal with.

Well, the meeting went well. They seemed to be receptive. I ended up calling in Tim and he did talk to his parents. Will there be resolution? I don't know. They now are aware of different happenings. They now are aware that they must all reach out, that they must share, that it is okay to disagree, but to let people know that you disagree. They are aware that they are all a family and they have to learn to work as a unit, to work through their issues, to think with their hearts and heads, and to include Tim in discussions. They must do these things if they are to make Tim progress from being the invisible boy to the visible one.

***

Who has the Power?

A young man came to see me the other day. Actually his parents suggested strongly that he do so and had me call him in. Reluctantly he entered my portals. It seems his grades last year were not reflective of his ability; he wasn't listening to suggestions at home. Indeed, he clearly had selected hearing and it did not include the voices of his parents. Looking at him, I wondered if his hearing would include my voice.

Well, we got talking or rather I got talking. Scott was not forthcoming with his responses. Probing, as I do, I found that he loved soccer and was a member of the team.

"Scott, tell me, when you are playing offense, are you just going to stand there, or are you going to go after the ball and try to score?"

He looked at me and laughed and said, "Of course I am going to try to score. Why else would I be on offense?"

"O.K.," I retorted, "then tell me, why don't you try to score in the classroom, too? You are sitting there, so why not do something?"

He thought for a moment, then looked at me and smiled.

"Get my drift?" I asked with a smile on my face, since I knew that he had.

We then segued into talking about his parents, two lovely people who just wanted him to succeed, but in wishing that, they seemed to always be in Scott's face. They truly felt they had the power to make him change; however, they were finding out that they didn't.

As parents you do want things to work out. You have a blueprint for your child and want him to be constructed according to plan, but alas, you just don't have that power. You cannot make things happen without the child's consent. If Scott doesn't want to do it, he won't and the more you cajole him, the less he will do. He wants to do it according to his own wishes, not yours, and just to be perverse, he won't do it if you are in his face. Sounds weird, huh? Yet, it happens every day. Scott wants to feel grown up. He wants to take responsibility for his actions. He wants the power and doesn't want to relinquish it to you. In fact he does have the power. He is the one who can make the changes; he is the one who can alter his actions; he is the one who has to have the desire to change.

As a parent, once you realize who really has the power it doesn't become all about you; it becomes all about Scott. And you know what? It does take a big load off of your shoulders. I mean you can't really sweat what you don't have the power to change. Shift the responsibility to where it belongs. Hand it over to Scott; give him the power. Make him responsible. You might be surprised. This will give him a sense of worth. He will reassess what he has done with his life and now seek to change.

Power empowers and that's what you will witness. Yes, you can give suggestions, but only he has the power to decide to follow them.

***

Constructive and Destructive Criticism

Put-Downs

Liz walks into my office. It is a sunny day outside, but her look clearly does not reflect the weather! "Mrs. Cohen, I am so sick of everyone putting me down. Like the teachers find fault with my work, my so-called friends snicker when I give an incorrect answer and my parents think I'm stupid. I'm beginning to think they're right."

And with that, Liz begins to cry. She is one sad gal whose self-esteem is at an all time low.

Talking in a quiet, soothing voice, I ask her to tell me exactly what is happening at home. Many times I find that things that occur at home are internalized, and color the meanings of statements made outside of the home. As we continued our discussion, I realized I was on target.

Actually, her parents were not the openly accusatory culprits; her sister was the one who constantly put her down. Her parents, however, were bystanders; rather than telling big sister to watch what she was saying, they allowed her to continue her put-downs, figuring that the two sisters could resolve their own issues. Obviously, this was not happening. However, now that I knew older sister was the perpetrator, I was able to zero in on the problem.

"Liz, how does Jane do in school?"

Looking at me, she responded, "Mrs. Cohen, her grades have not been good and she has been grounded for not completing her homework."

"And how does that make her feel?" I ask.

Naturally, the grounding has made her big sister furious. She looks around, sees her seemingly happy sister, and decides that she, Jane, needs some company in the unhappy and miserable department. After all, misery loves company. I explain these thoughts to Liz, telling her that those who are unhappy about themselves usually deliver put-downs. They really dislike seeing someone else who is happy. So, Jane wants to make Liz unhappy, too.

Liz discusses her schoolwork with me and I point out to her that she is doing pretty well. Actually, she is doing nicely in most of her subjects. Since she seems to crave kudos, I make certain I deliver many. Math is giving her some problems, but she is going for help. Her math teacher is not picking on her; rather, she has been pointing out the mistakes that Liz has been making and has been suggesting that she correct them. Liz, because she is already upset with her sister, perceives the teacher's suggestions as put-downs. She feels whenever anyone tells her something, even if it is constructive, that they are picking on her.

Next, we examine her friends whom she thinks have been snickering at her. Through further discussion Liz begins to see that they, too, are not really picking at her; rather, they are laughing with her. Because Liz was so upset with her sister, she wrongfully felt her friends were putting her down, too.

I suggest to Liz that I call her parents to let them know how she is feeling. Liz leaves my office, with her head held a little higher. She even gives me a smile. At least she finally feels that maybe something will be done and she has managed to unburden herself a little bit through sharing with me.

I make a telephone call to Mom. Mom explains that she was trying to let the girls settle their own differences, and did not realize the impact Jane's remarks were making on Liz. I lauded Mom for allowing the girls to attempt to work things out by themselves, but told her that sometimes a parent has to step in.

It behooves Mom and Dad to put a stop to Jane's barbs and to let Liz know that her parents are proud of her academic achievement in most of her classes. Big sister Jane is the one who must do some soul-searching. She must take ownership of her problems. She must start focusing on herself, not on her younger sister. Instead of using so much energy to put down her sister, Jane should use that energy to lift up herself.

When put-downs happen, analyze them. Who is issuing them? What is the reason for them? Are the reasons based in fact? If your children are on the receiving end, find out why. Talk to your children. If it is feasible, meet with the perpetrators of the put-downs. Together, do try to solve the problem.

***

Bully for You

It must have been almost 20 years ago, but I remember it as if it were yesterday. I was walking down one of the school's corridors when all of a sudden I saw this big bruiser lift this small boy up in the air and pin him against the wall. Talking to him in a mocking tone, he was clearly threatening him and/or warning him about something.

Filled with anger and horror, I marched forward, and yelled, "Put him down this instant."

Incredibly, the bully did just that. The victim, clearly shaken, moved behind me and the perpetrator was given a stern look and told to report to my office.

Can you imagine how much bullying goes on that we do not know about? Can you imagine the impact the bullying makes upon the victim? How can we recognize these bullies? What makes them bullies? What can be done to protect others from them?

Bullying is any ongoing physical or verbal mistreatment where someone has amazing power over someone else and takes out negative action on the victim. Just who is a bully? Usually, children who bully need to control and dominate others and do this through verbal threats and physical actions. A bully often perceives that the world revolves around him. Often, he is physically larger than others his age. At times, he has misperceptions and sees himself as a victim. He will assume that someone did not bump into him accidentally; rather, the person did it on purpose. Therefore, in his mind, if the bully chooses to retaliate, that is justified.

At times, bullies are simply mimicking what they have seen occur at home. If they see an aggressive parent in action, they figure that gives them license to be aggressive. They are very angry and need to vent. Instead of venting in a positive fashion, they choose to bully.

Some bullies do have low self-esteem and want others to feel the same way they do, so they decide to inflict pain on the others and make them suffer. Some of them have "teammates" who egg and cheer them on; many times they ask these "teammates" to do their dirty work, while the bullies just look on.

If you hear that your child is bullying someone or if you see bullying behavior exhibited at home, what can you do as a parent? Really take a close look at your youngster. Do you know his friends? Do you notice if he watches movies filled with aggression? Do you ask him how things are going at school with his peer group? Do you emphasize the positive that your child is doing in order to improve his self-esteem? Do you point out to him how the victim must feel? Do you take a good look at your own home surroundings and question how secure and loved your child feels? Do you really listen to your child and help him deal with frustration in a timely and positive fashion? Do you tolerate bullying behavior? Do you mete out appropriate punishment when rules are not respected and practiced?

Bullying is learned behavior; it can be unlearned.

***

"Sticks and stones will break my bones but names will never hurt me"

Remember this chant? We said it, but did we believe it? No! Names did hurt us. And they are continuing to hurt victims of bullying today. Just who are these victims and what can be done to help them?

Usually, the typical victim is physically weaker than his peers and is quiet, sensitive, shy, cautious, and often withdrawn. Many times, he will feel that he cannot control his environment, blames himself for his problems, has low self-esteem and has poor interpersonal skills. Many times he is immature, has overprotective parents and has not learned how to fend for himself. Clearly, he does not portray a threat to his attacker. A matter of fact, he looks like easy prey.

As an outsider, it is hard to find out who the victim is since invariably he is embarrassed to come forward or feels, because of his low self-esteem, that the bullying is warranted. Once the victim is identified, how can he be helped? It is important to encourage peer involvement. Once he has friends, he will no longer be such an easy target. Tell the victim that he should try to ignore the bully. When this is impossible, he should move away from the bully, tell him to stop, and seek out advice and help from an adult.

Do not tell your child to fight back. You will just be reinforcing negative aggressive behavior. Do try to get your child to talk about the bullying. Make certain your child knows that he is O.K.; he is not a bad person; he is not deserving of the abuse. Stress his positive attributes.

Encourage your child to get involved in school activities. Many victims are loners; once they become involved, their victimization ceases. Help your child develop his talents. Praise him. Go to some functions in which he is involved. If your child is experiencing bouts of depression, if he is feeling really blue, do seek out the advice of a trained professional counselor. Once your child feels better about himself, the insults will not bother him. He will feel good about himself and not buy into the negative barbs that are thrown his way. When the bully no longer receives attention, the bullying will stop. The victim will no longer be considered easy prey. His aura of self-confidence will shine through and discourage the bully.

Each child has the right to embrace his life and to lead it in a safe environment where he can securely spread his wings, explore and grow. If the safe environment is sullied by the actions of a bully, the bully should be identified and stopped. Therefore, encourage your child to share any mistreatment with you.

This is not a sign of tattling. Actually, he is helping himself and other students who may be victims, too. Moreover, he is helping the bully by having his misbehavior identified and hopefully positively changed.

***

Mirrors

Each day I look into a mirror; although I must be honest. I don't like doing it too often. What happened to the dark brown hair? What are those lines I see? The figure doesn't look like it did a few years ago. What's going on? I have to tell myself that mirrors do not lie. They are true reflections of me. And that got me thinking about reflections and mirrors.

Think of reflections…kids are really reflections of us parents. What they do, how they think, sometimes their looks…all of these reflect the parents with whom they live. So what about us as parents?

We must come to the realization that our children see what we are doing, often internalize it, and then mirror those actions. If they see us coming home and having a drink to relax, they figure it's O.K. for them to have a drink or use some other things in order to relax. After all, if parents, their mentors can do it, they should be able to do it, too.

What about the kid who sees Mom and Dad yelling all the time? Often that kid mirrors those actions when he is dealing with his friends or teachers. To him, yelling is the way to make his wants known.

What about the child who sees physical abuse in the family? Many times that youngster will start fighting in school, start abusing a boyfriend or girlfriend, and not feel that much remorse. He sees the behavior at home, internalizes it, and makes it his own.

What about the child who hears constant complaining, who never hears that the glass is half full, but rather has to listen to how empty it is all the time? What feelings does he take with him? Will he be optimistic or pessimistic as he goes through the day? Believe it or not, depression and pessimism are contagious. It's hard to be joyful in gloomy surroundings.

What about the child who sees parents get easily frustrated doing a task? The parents give up and say, "Why bother?" and then go on to something else.

38

What does this teach the child about perseverance? What does it teach him about asking for help or asking for explanations?

What about the youngster who hears parents blame their bosses for their troubles or perhaps blame their acquaintances for their troubles? In other words, they blame anyone but themselves for their misfortunes. Does this allow the youngster to take responsibility for his actions or does it enable him to blame others and feel O.K. about doing this?

What about the kid who is the butt of constant put-downs? No matter what he tries to do, he is put down by a parent, rather than praised. Moreover, he hears one parent constantly putting down another. How is this child going to feel? What will his self-esteem be like?

As your children look into the mirrors, what do you want them to see? How about love, understanding and compassion for starters? Be mindful of what the mirror reflects. Positive reflections, or negative reflections…as parents, the choice is yours.

***

Reach Out and Touch Someone

As part of an ongoing Jewish/Black dialogue, I had the good fortune of visiting a Baptist church. I say good fortune because the service left me with such a good feeling and I found I was in wonderful spirits for the rest of the day. I've been to synagogues and other churches, but the feelings of warmth and goodwill have never surrounded me as much as they had on that Sunday. Actually, the religion was alien to me, yet I still embraced the feelings I found. Why did that happen?

Musing on the events of that morning, I realized that I felt such warmth because my husband and I were not isolated beings. Yes, we were seated together on the pew with others, like we would be at other services. Yet, the people around us did not just look ahead at the Minister; instead, they looked at us, smiled and greeted us warmly with a handshake. Indeed, they literally reached out and touched us.

During the service, the Minister reached out and touched us, too, with his words of welcome, prayer, and sharing, as did the beautiful men's choir whose music caressed us and enveloped us with its warmth. As the songs were sung, we were invited to join in. We didn't know some of the words, but they were fed to us by one of the choir members. He reached out to us and encouraged us to join in. We sang heartily and loudly, clapped our hands, and felt our spirits rise.

As I looked around, young and old were singing; we were performing as one. Our voices had joined as one. Our skin tones were different, but those were just our outer trappings; our inner trappings were the same. We all needed and projected love, warmth, and caring.

The choir from our temple performed, too, and those in attendance, although they did not know the words, could feel the spirit of them and were caught up in the cadence and sound of the rich voices. One church member started clapping in time to the music; soon others joined in. Now, Black and White alike were connected and responding.

After the service had gone on for a while, the Minister invited all of us to get up, walk around the room and greet each other. What a feeling I derived as I was warmly greeted, embraced, and welcomed by members of the church community! Young, old, male, and female all reached out to welcome my husband and me. The piano was being played, but we needed no music since there was already music in our hearts and souls.

Once seated, our Rabbi was invited to speak. As he preached, I looked around and noticed everyone was paying rapt attention. During one of the Rabbi's salient points, a parishioner behind me yelled out, "Right on, brother!" How those words got to me! Yes, regardless of our skin, we are all brothers and sisters.

Just before the service ended, we were asked to join hands with everyone present, so that there was almost a continuous ring around the room. Then, we prayed and sang together. We were connected as human beings and how beautiful it was!

The message I took home with me that Sunday has stayed with me. It is a powerful and meaningful one; one that I know does make a difference. As I saw during the service, a life can be so positively changed by simply remembering to reach out and touch someone. Don't wait until a service to make this happen. Start today; you'll feel better and so will those whose lives you have touched.

***

The Clean Slate

Yesterday, I was in a store and saw some little babies sleeping peacefully in carriages. Later, I saw another baby who was wide-awake, peering around, and seemingly content. How innocent! How hopeful! How secure! I began to muse about a baby's being and what happens as that baby grows.

Looking at the same child at four, what would I see? Perhaps I would see a child displaying fits of anger; perhaps I would see a child filled with a sunny disposition; perhaps I would see a child filled with boldness; perhaps I would see a child filled with shyness. Why would there be such variations?

I think this is because a child is like a clean slate. There are no marks on the slate until certain interactions take place. Then, its appearance is forever altered; each mark leaves its impression upon the slate and adds to the overall effect. Let's look at two of my students to see what I mean.

Susie was born with a clean slate into a home of caring parents. Her wants were met, love was bestowed, and she received a lot of positive reinforcements. Yes, she did receive discipline, but it was always accompanied by love. Since her slate was being imprinted with positive marks, her countenance clearly reflected that fact. When she went to school, she was quick to raise her hand and voice her opinions. Her teachers were encouraging and used a lot of positive reinforcements. She interacted well with her peers. Yes, Susie's slate had good marks; it had acceptance, love, and a wonderful sense of self.

Steve, like Susie, was born with a clean slate; however, he was brought home to a house that was filled with discord. His parents and siblings were always shouting. He found he had to make a lot of noise in order to be heard and get their attention. When he went to school, he would speak out in class even when he was not addressed. On the playground, he would fight with the other pupils. He wanted his own way and was not willing to make any compromises. Of course his behavior caused others to avoid him and this just intensified his anger and negativity. In class he would take it personally when the teacher would try to correct him. Unfortunately, his slate was being filled with such negativity that he was projecting that to everyone around him. Unlike Susie, Steve was not on a good path. Unless the negatives could be erased from his slate and the positives added, Steve would continue to be an unhappy camper. Eventually he would display more anger or his anger would be turned inward and he would become depressed.

These scenarios show clearly how important it is for all those with whom children come in contact to remember that they are putting marks on the children's slates, marks that will affect and alter the course of their lives. Therefore, it is important that they imprint with care. What is written on a chalkboard can be erased; what is imprinted on a child often lasts forever.

***

Validation

My husband and I were leaving a parking lot the other day and reached for our ticket that had been validated. Giving it to the attendant, we were able to exit the parking lot without paying. As we continued driving along, I began to ponder the word validate and realized how important it is not only to enable you to park free, but also to enable you to lead a healthy and happy life.

Validate means to support or confirm. Think about a person on a job. It is nice to be validated.

It makes one feel warm and good to have the boss come over and say, "Hey, Joe, I just wanted to tell you that you're doing a super job. Keep up the good work!"

You smile outwardly and inwardly. Not only do you feel good, but also you feel energized to roll up your shirtsleeves and strive to do even better in your work. You have been recognized; you have been confirmed as a human being. You are not just a number; you have a face that is recognized by the boss and your services have been acknowledged.

In addition to having one's deed validated, it's important to have one's thoughts and ideas recognized as well. Perhaps your ideas are not really going to be able to work, but at least they should be allowed to be aired, to initially be validated, and to be supported. In this way, you will feel important. You will be encouraged to speak up further, to offer more suggestions and to realize that you have worth.

Students in school should be validated often. It has been shown that through encouragement often comes success. Yes, we all do make mistakes and these should be recognized, but so should the good deeds we do and the thoughts that we share.

Imagine if every time we opened our mouths, we were told that our ideas were ridiculous. After a while, we would stop sharing ideas since we would not want to be put down all the time. Lack of validation causes lack of growth. It fosters a "why bother" attitude.

That's why it's so important for a teacher to not only give constructive criticism, but also to give support and confirmation.

"Terri, your grammar needs some improvement, but your basic ideas are excellent."

Now Terri does not feel that the whole paper is horrible; instead, she has been encouraged to expand upon her good ideas and work on her grammar.

Validation works well at home, too. If a parent keeps finding fault with his youngster, the youngster may stop doing anything. It's sort of like a fighter in a ring. If he constantly is punched and knocked down, after a while he just won't bother to get up.

Let's take a look at John. He just never seems to get anything done around the house. His room should be condemned! Instead of just screaming at him and telling him that you don't live in a pigpen, say something positive.

"John, you always look terrific when you're dressed and ready for school. Your car, too, is so neat inside. I'm proud of how nicely you keep it. Let's see if you can start keeping your room neat and clean, too."

Now, instead of picking on him unmercifully for his pigsty, you have validated him for some positive happening and in that way have encouraged him to start thinking about his room.

Validation is so important. We all need some to continue to grow as happy and healthy human beings.

***

Warm Fuzzies

Remember when you were a little kid sitting in third grade and the teacher stood in the front of the classroom holding a bunch of papers. Looking though the papers, she stopped, selected one, held it up for all to see and told everyone that this particular paper was done perfectly. Then she told the class that you had done it. Immediately you felt your chest swell with pride. Wow! You felt good!

When you went home, you couldn't wait to share the good news with your parents. You waved the paper at your folks and they enthusiastically praised you and gave the paper a place of honor on the refrigerator. For the rest of the day and night you gloated.

As you got older, the accolades lessened. Good work wasn't applauded; it was expected. Lousy work was noted…noted with red marks on your paper, noted with disapproving glances from the teacher and your peers and noted by you who had a creeping feeling of despair.

When your schooling was done, you entered the work place. Again, good work was expected, not praised. If you stayed late, no one praised you, but if you arrived late, you heard about it! You completed an assignment, felt an inward glow of satisfaction and eagerly handed the assignment to your boss who accepted it, kind of muttered a thank you and that was it. Deflated, you walked away.

Why does praise seem to stop as we age? We are still people; we still need and want those warm fuzzies. Yes, they can come internally, we can praise ourselves, but we feel much better when someone on the outside praises us. In fact, it often makes us work harder. When we're not praised, we may feel, "Why bother? Who cares anyway?"

It's strange. I know my husband loves me, but every once in a while I like to have him bring home some flowers…just because. Even though I am not a kid anymore, I still love warm fuzzies and surprises.

I can't count the number of times I have asked a kid in my office if his parents ever praised him. Often the answer is no. He hears about disapproval, but not about approval. What happened to the gold stars that used to be freely given to the young? The teenager and the adult still need those stars to blossom and grow.

Praise is essential to a person's well being so do not be afraid to heap on the accolades when they are warranted.

***

I'm Proud of You

Today as I continued to see students who have been having difficulty in their classes, I realized that I often put those who are doing well on the back burner. They are succeeding, so I figure they are doing just fine without my intervention.

Yet, maybe I am really doing them a disservice. Kids who are succeeding still need pats on the back.

When you think about it…what do we notice? That's easy…the mistakes. When papers are handed back from the teacher, we notice the red marks on them, not the other words that are left untouched. When we commit an error, it really gives us pause and we strongly remember it.

I remember my children bringing home report cards. Looking them over, my eyes settled first on those grades that I felt could be raised and those are the ones I talked to them about. Yet, there may have been other grades that were all super and I didn't give those as much emphasis even though the boys had deserved praise for the good work that they had done in those areas.

So, when I called Mike into my office because of his progress reports, I decided to concentrate on the whole picture. We talked about all his subjects. We spoke about the sports that he does and the many accolades that he has received. We spoke about his work outside of school and his hobbies. Then, we tackled the negative reports. Instead of really berating him, I listened to why he had received them and what he was planning to do about them. I noticed that instead of getting defensive, Mike was positive and shared with me his reasons and his concerns. Together, we even came up with a good game plan on how to improve the grades that were not up to par.

Because I did not put him on the defensive, he was so much more receptive than the students to whom I had spoken earlier. Actually, he didn't even make excuses and try to blame his lousy grades on anyone but himself. He didn't have to. I was not lecturing; I was listening.

When we discussed the good grades, sports awards, etc., I told him how proud I was of him and I could almost see him light up with joy; his face was actually beaming. Naturally, he felt chagrined about his negative marks, but I hadn't just focused on those. By looking at the total picture, I was looking at the total Mike and not making him feel like a failure. In truth, he wasn't a failure; he had accomplished many good things. Now, he just had to put more effort into certain areas.

How easy it is for all of us to find fault, yet how difficult it often is to praise! Next time progress reports are issued, remember to look at the total picture. Where appropriate, the following words can work wonders…"I'm proud of you!"

***

Positive Mental Attitude

I gotta tell you, from my many years' experience of dealing with people, I have seen that a major ticket to success is a positive mental attitude.

Actually, I even heard about it when I was a little kid. My folks read me that little classic, *The Little Engine That Could* and as they read the story to me, I could almost feel the energy that the engine needed in order to make it up the mountain. He kept saying, "I think I can, I think I can, I think I can" almost in mantra form...and you know what, he made it! I reflect, too, about the story of the tortoise and the hare. Even though the tortoise was slower, in his mind he felt that he could beat the hare and he did!

While I watched the Olympics, I was struck by the sheer determination seen in each participant's eyes. You could sense the intense focus and the keen desire to win. Without those ingredients, the skill could be there, but it would not have played out so magnificently.

What about the high school athlete and/or student? It's amazing to watch some of the athletes. I remember this one boy who would do beautifully during each practice, but then when he entered the "field of battle", he would freeze and not be able to perform to the best of his ability.

I think, too, of the girl who came to see me obviously distraught. She couldn't understand how her grades could be so good and her SAT scores could be so low. Talking about the situation, I ascertained that she would get very nervous before each test. She knew how well she had to do, would tense up, and all the words, especially in the reading passages, would seem to blur. She would desperately try to make sense out of them. Panic would set in, she would tell herself that she was going to score badly and that's exactly what did happen when she received her scores!

Amazing isn't it! We have these thoughts about not doing well and they come true. Why? I really think that people who don't have a high self-esteem are the ones plagued by this the most. Inwardly, they feel that they are going to do poorly; they tense up, and their worst fears become realities. Instead of having a positive mental attitude and using the mantra of the little engine, they use their own negative mantra and find they can't!!!

Pondering this for a moment, I think back to the days when I used to play on a tennis team. All night long, I would twist and turn, thinking about the game-to-be. In the morning, I would be exhausted from anxiety. Once on the court, my

What a difference! I can almost see Jen smiling as she reads the comments. The teacher has encouraged, not discouraged. Now Jen will feel good about herself and look forward to applying herself even more diligently to her next test.

You know, it is always so easy to find fault, to pick out the things that should be circled in red. We tend to dwell on the negatives instead of the positives, but in so doing, what are we doing to our children? We are discouraging them from trying harder. If they are constantly put down, many feel why bother! But, if we choose to look at the positives and reinforce them, then we build up our children's self- confidence and encourage them to perform even better.

***

Why Won't He Ever Praise Me?

I kept calling Ann into my office; however, she never came. Actually, I wasn't surprised; rather, I was annoyed and frustrated. Ann is a senior and her grades are not good. To make matters worse, she wasn't even coming to school regularly, so she had a lot of work to make up and time was running out. What to do?

Finally word got to me that Ann was in school. Instead of sending her a pass, I went into her classroom almost at the end of class, quietly asked the teacher if I could talk to Ann in my office, and then sought out Ann and together we walked down the hall to my office.

During the walk, she seemed her usual giggly self, "Hey, I bet you want to see me about graduation. Don't worry; I'll make it. I'm here today, right?" and with that she gave another nervous giggle.

Once in my office, I took out her report card. I find when the facts are laid out in black and white, it's hard to deny them. Ann looked at them, they were no surprise, but she still insisted she would make it.

I said, "Do you realize that you have missed almost half of school? How can you pass a subject if you are not there to hear what the teacher has to say? What's the deal?"

"Nothing," came her reply.

Not willing to take that as an answer, I looked at her quizzically and said, "Wrong! It must be something. No one chooses to just stay out of school. No one really wants to get lousy grades. Ann, your report card can't make you feel happy and proud of yourself when you look at it. Right?"

As Ann had done in the hallway, she gave another nervous giggle and added a few comments. Outwardly, she tried to put on a very cavalier attitude. She wanted me to lay off her and to think that everything would really be O.K. Swell, but I wasn't biting! Not this time.

I decided to stop questioning her on her grades and to ask her questions about home, about her family, about any possible problems and concerns.

Initially, she had this big grin on her face and looked at me incredulously.

"Anything wrong at my house? You must be kidding. All is fine."

I continued, "Tell me about Dad. What does he think about your grades?"

Immediately, I saw a change in her demeanor. Her blue eyes darkened.

She said, "Well, you know, he's your typical man. He just doesn't care! I mean he sits in front of the TV with a beer in his hand and it's like I don't exist, unless of course I do something to annoy him. Or even if I don't do something to annoy him, he just starts yelling at me."

The torrent of words stopped and Ann took a breath.

Now was my chance to interject and looking directly at her, I said, "Ann, not all men are like that. Does Dad hit you?"

She told me that he doesn't hit her; he just provides emotional abuse with his yelling. He yells at her mother, too, who just quietly takes it and figures, like always, the storm will pass. Ann told me that she just goes up to her room when Dad yells. She shuts the door to subconsciously shut out not only his words, but also that part of her life.

"Oh, Ann, I am so sorry. It must be hard for you."

The tears started rolling down her cheeks.

In a halting voice she continued, "Mrs. Cohen, no one cares if I pass or fail, really. I mean Mom just wants to survive and Dad just seems to yell at me for everything, bad grades or not. He never praises me. In fact, he really doesn't seem to notice I exist. And then, all of a sudden, I realize he does, cuz he starts to yell.

You know, sometimes, I just lay awake at night and wonder why I am so bad. Why must he yell at me? How can I be better? How can I walk around the house so he will maybe not notice me?"

From our conversation, I realized that Ann probably does not come to school on some days because she is just so tired. She must really feel sick from fatigue and worry and just can't get out of bed.

When I asked her if she has discussed the situation with her mother, she told me that she has.

"But Dad yells at her, too. Mom tells me to just stay out of his way. She told me she has learned to live with his abuse. She doesn't have a decent job, and he provides the money to give us food and a roof over our heads. Sometimes, Mom told me, you just got to do what you have to do. I try to listen to her, Mrs. Cohen, but it's getting so hard to put up with Dad's yelling."

We talked about Ann's survival techniques. I suggested that perhaps she wears a smile on her face all the time so people won't get to see the real Ann. When I asked her if she has many friends she told me that she really doesn't like to get too close to anyone. She has friends, but no one to whom she's a best friend. If she gets too close to anyone, they will find out that she has problems.

"Ann," I said, "You have put a wall around you to protect you from Dad's screaming. In doing so you have kept others at arm's length, too. And if they don't know what's troubling you, they can't help you."

"But, Mrs. Cohen, why won't he ever praise me? I do some nice things, you know and for what. He never notices."

Looking at her, I gently responded. "Ann, he's probably a very unhappy guy. He can't yell at work or he would lose his job, so he yells at home where he feels safe, and he chooses to yell at the two people who are close to him – you and Mom. You both don't yell back, you walk on eggshells so that you don't upset him, so in a way, you enable him to continue. There are no consequences for his actions, so he feels safe in yelling. Ann, you're not the one at fault. You're not a bad person. Dad is the one who must work out his problems, but will that happen, I don't know. I know, though, that you must start believing in yourself, and start believing that you are a worthwhile person. You know, by coming to school, by bringing up your grades, you will be able to graduate, go on to school or get a job. Then, you'll be able to move out of your house, and go on with your life."

Will Ann be able to truly go on? Will she really be able to develop a feeling of trust for another person? Will she start to feel better about herself? Will she be able to separate the fact that she can love her dad, but dislike his actions? Then, too, will Dad ever wake up from his misery and be able to reach out to others with respect and love? Will he ever praise her? I don't know. But I hope so.

***

Criticism

How often have you told your youngster something only to receive the following retort, "Stop criticizing me! You're not perfect either, you know!" However, when we criticize others and they criticize us, we are not thinking about perfection. Rather, we are simply pointing something out what we feel needs sharing.

Ah, but here's the problem. Our criticism is taken personally. Instead of realizing we are criticizing an idea or an action, the object of the criticism feels we are criticizing the whole person.

How can we criticize without creating unhappiness for ourselves and others? Perhaps the best way is for all parties concerned to see criticism as a tool for growth, rather than a weapon of attack. Actually, criticism is a way to provide some valuable information. Just make certain that the information is constructive. It must be meant to help and improve. It must not be destructive; that tears down and hurts. When criticizing, you should always give a prelude and tell why you are sharing the information. Never talk in put-downs. Remember, too, to keep your voice at an even level; if you yell, the listener will yell and vice-versa.

Let's look at the scenario of the kid who comes home from school and feels he is unfairly criticized all the time. What can you as a parent do? It really doesn't help to say, "You must be imagining this." Instead, tell the youngster that if he doesn't agree with the criticism, then he won't be hurt by it since he doesn't have to own it. Before he gets all uptight, he must consider the source. If a friend is criticizing him about the way he swings a bat and the friend has never before played ball, then how valid is the friend's criticism?

Sometimes criticism is deserved. Once the youngster is able to get his ego under control, it becomes easier for him to listen to criticism. In fact, criticism can give him some valuable insight. He may have wondered why so and so is angry with him. Perhaps it's because he has a sarcastic way of speaking, but he doesn't realize it. By making him aware, he is now in a position to change.

Sometimes criticism is troublesome because we are not all coming from the same place. The mother who angrily says to her son, "Your room looks like a cyclone. Clean it up. We're not living in a barn!" may be seeing the room differently from how her son perceives it.

Instead of accusing your son of being a slob, you should sit down and discuss with him what he thinks his room should look like. Then, share with him how you feel it should look and come to a meeting of the minds. Explain to him that if his clothes are not put away or put into the hamper, soon he will have no clean clothes to wear. By sharing the reasons behind the criticism, you make the criticism understandable and easier to handle.

Remember, criticism is never easy to accept. It is often humiliating to have others point out your shortcomings. Yet, being confronted with a bit of truth can be a big help. So, instead of reacting in a negative fashion to criticism, the person criticized should seek out the truth behind it, something to validate the criticism. Then, as the cliché goes, "If the shoe fits, wear it!"

Yes, it is O.K. to criticize where warranted. But it is important to always criticize with love. Remember, too, just as you deserve to be able to criticize so does your child as long as the criticism is valid and followed by reasons.

Next time criticism must occur, try to think of it as a suggestion and share it in a caring fashion. Be open to dialogue about your suggestion and be willing to defend and discuss your stance.

Remember, criticism is good when it is constructive; criticism is counterproductive when it is destructive.

***

Choices

Everything we do is actually a choice…what will we choose and why?

Choices

The word "choices" has been ringing in my mind lately. Students are coming in to see me about their postgraduate plans. Have they picked the right school? Should they go to work or to college? Should they live away from home? **CHOICES**

A student comes into my office. He's failing a course. Should he drop it or hang in there? **CHOICES**

A divorced parent calls me on the phone. Her child wishes to move from one parent's home to another, from one community to another. Should the child move or stay? **CHOICES**

A child in the parking lot starts harassing another child. A third student witnesses this. Should he intervene? Should he tell an administrator, teacher, or parent? **CHOICES**

A teacher has rules for the class. Mitigating circumstances have occurred that could allow the teacher to make an exception in the case of a student. Should this be done? **CHOICES**

Vacation time is coming for a husband, yet it begins before school vacation. It's a rare occurrence when the family can spend quality time together. But the student should be attending school. What to do? **CHOICES**

A girl is at a party. She's feeling uptight and shy. She looks at her friend who is having a wonderful time laughing and talking with everyone. Another person approaches her and offers her some weed…guaranteed, she is told, to make her have fun, too. Should she take it? **CHOICES**

A person is working in a job. Each day he comes home tired, upset, and frazzled. Yet, the money is needed. Should he quit? Should he stay? Should he seek other options? **CHOICES**

I could go on and on, but I think you get the picture. All of life is made up of choices. How we deal with those choices directly affects our lives. It is important to realize that every choice has a consequence. Do we want to own and wear that consequence? **CHOICES**

If we choose to just keep putting off making a decision, making a choice, then the problem will continue. We can choose to be part of the problem or part of the solution. The **CHOICE** is ours.

No one can really make us choose anything without our consent, but once we consent to the choice, it's ours. What if it's a bad choice? I always tell my students that from every choice there is a consequent learning experience. If the choice is a bad one, at least they've learned that; then, they are able to regroup and make a different choice.

The main thing to remember is that we must make choices. Life is about choices. If we do not choose to make choices, we stay stagnant, we often stay unhappy, we feel stuck…but after all, aren't we really making the **CHOICE** to be that way?

***

Teamwork

When you really think about it no one stands completely alone. We are all on this planet together. That's probably why whatever we do invariably affects someone else, too. Because of that, I think it's important to remember that we are all part of a team. And being part of a team means that we have to realize that everything is not just about us. Others are involved, too, and we must think of them.

As a student, if you talk out a lot in class, you will be disruptive to those around you and will interfere with their learning process. Likewise, if you yell out all the answers and don't give anyone else a chance, then you are precluding them from taking an active part in the class. If you are playing a sport, basketball for instance, and choose to hog the ball, not only will you get exhausted, but also you will not be allowing others to get in on the plays, you will not be allowing them to hone or share their skills. Because of resultant fatigue, you may actually be hurting the team and missing a lot of shots that could have been made if others were in on the plays.

As a parent, it is important, too, to realize that you are part of a team. Learn not to just dictate, but to allow for discussion. Learn to include others, regardless of age, in your conversation. In this way, everyone will feel important. And when people are allowed to participate, they take an active interest and work harder at making the team work. Don't be afraid to ask your child to help you around the house. After all, you all live there together. He may grumble a little, but by helping, he will be taking on responsibility, will become a viable part of the family unit and will eventually take pride in what he has accomplished.

If a child is on a sports team, he knows how important it is to work together to make the team be the best that it can be.

I always look at kids in a huddle and think, "This is so good. Look how the huddle brings everyone together and enables them to actually visualize and feel that they are working as a unit."

Being in a circle connects one to the other; there is no beginning or end. It is continuous, filled with a never-ending flow of energy and support. Yes, it is a team.

Think about an orchestra. It is a group effort; it is not just about the individual, but also about all the individuals coming together to create beautiful music. If one person is out of sync, the performance will not be a good one. Think about cheerleading. When the people are lifted up, if those on the bottom are not doing their job, the others will fall. The ones on the bottom will have let down the team and the routine will have been ruined.

Think of parents. Even if parents are divorced, it is so much better if they act as a team. They should not be giving their children mixed messages. They should be supportive of each other and function as a unit. Otherwise, children will not know what to do. They will not have received clear-cut messages. They will not feel secure because the team...the parenting team...would not have been acting as a whole.

As is apparent, it is so important to choose to work as a team. Our load will be lighter, more things will be accomplished, communication will be easier, and friendships will be forged and solidified. More inclusion means more involvement, so reach out and make those with whom you come in contact become members of your team. Remember, we are all on this planet together.

***

The Palette of Life

Let's take a look at a rainbow of colors and see what each one means in our lives.

Red- think how we hear it used...one turns red with embarrassment; one is red in the face; one is seeing red. Yes, we feel anger at times and that is not a bad thing. Anger gets the adrenaline flowing, gets us to take action and gets us to examine our feelings. Why do we have anger? What can we do about it? We must act on our anger in order to feel better; however, it is important to count to 10 or maybe even 20 before we react so that we will have some time to chill out and respond more appropriately.

Blue…that's what happens to us if we don't vent our feelings. We become blue. We become depressed. Nothing seems exciting to us. It is hard to get moving. Perhaps it is hard to focus and concentrate. We dwell on our problems, yet we are unable to react. That's why it is better to see red, then to feel blue. It is better to vent, than to keep everything bottled up inside of us.

Yellow…this really has two meanings and they seem to be opposite from each other. Yellow is often used to suggest someone who is scared, someone who is afraid to react. We may be meek and mild mannered; we may be afraid of getting into the fray of life. By staying on the sidelines, we are missing so much. We should try to confront our fears and venture forth. By pushing ourselves a little, we will find that it isn't as bad or as scary as we thought. And with new opportunities to experience, we will be broadened and strengthened.

Yellow also connotes sunshine. It connotes brightness. It connotes optimism. It is so important to try to have an optimistic outlook on life. If we portray a happy countenance, others will greet us in a similar fashion. After all, laughter and a positive mental attitude are contagious. They infect all those around us. People will seek us out; they will want to be in our company. We will make them feel good. If we look at things positively, we will be able to be upbeat about what otherwise might have seemed insurmountable.

Black …although many like to wear black because it is slenderizing, the color actually denotes sadness, despair and gloominess. We are in a black mood. Nothing seems to be good. With a gloom and doom attitude, daily life is no fun. People will shun us; after all, our dark mood is catchy and who wants to feel miserable? There is a time for somberness, this is true, but to choose to wear black all the time is depressing and will isolate us from others and stop us from cheerfully completing tasks. Black is so similar to blue, although black is even more intense than blue. When our mood is totally black and has been that way for a while, perhaps we should think about seeking some medical advice.

White…this color denotes cleanliness and purity. That's probably why so many in the medical profession choose to don it. When we are neat and clean, we find we can perform better. When we are organized, our thoughts seem to be better organized. When we have pure thoughts, we are able to deal with them appropriately; we are able to see the situations clearly; they are not muddied with other trivia or other problems.

But white also means pale. You've heard the expression, "Pale as a ghost" or "White as a sheet". None of the other colors are in the picture; there is an absence of color. We are neither blue with unhappiness nor red with anger. We are neither yellow with delight or black with depression. We just are. And when that happens we have to search within ourselves and find meaning to our lives. We must involve ourselves in tasks that will renew us, that will embolden us with color so that we can shine again.

Green – this color means envy. And envy is something that we must strive to avoid. We should not covet our neighbor; rather, we should rejoice in what we have or strive hard to obtain things that we want. Envy just adds to discontent. It stunts our growth. We are so busy comparing ourselves to this one and that one and worrying that we don't match up and don't have what someone else has that we become stymied. In fact, we don't really move forward since we are consumed with jealously and this overshadows everything that we do possess causing us not to appreciate our own good fortune.

I have only touched on some of the colors. You may add others to your palette. What color will you choose to wear today? My wish is that you find yourselves "in the pink"!

***

Enabling

A mother comes into my office to discuss her son's performance in school. "Well, I just don't understand it. He really is a bright kid, but he does have this job now that he goes to right after school and he works until 9 PM, but he tells me he can get his work done in school."

Leaning forward, I say, "Did you tell him that if his grades go down, the job will have to cease?"

"No," she replied, "He told me he could handle everything and when I first saw that the grades were low, we did talk about it, but he promised me that he had everything under control and not to worry, so I didn't."

"Well," I say, "unfortunately, you have enabled your son to continue to get low grades."

The well-meaning mom looked at me dumbfounded. How many times do we think we're being good parents, but, in actuality, we are enabling behavior to continue?

Consider the following… if we wonder why our child has difficulty with decision-making, yet we make all the decisions for him, then we should reassess the situation and realize we are enabling. We must empower our children to take ownership of their own problems. In this way, **they** will take ownership of **their** decisions and consequences.

Think about discipline. If appropriate action is not taken at home or school to preclude the unwanted behavior, then it's almost a given that the negative behavior will continue. After all, why should it stop? Nothing was done to make the perpetrator stop and ponder his actions. It's important to recognize that by being too nice, we are not necessarily doing a child a favor.

Conjure up this image. A young child is learning to walk. Mom always holds his hand. Looking around at other children his age, Mom wonders why they are walking alone and hers needs assistance.

Upon asking a friend, she is told, "Do you ever leave your child's side, go across the room and call to him? I bet without your holding his hand, he'll try to walk to the other side of the room by himself."

You see, it's important to give your child space to walk alone, to not enable him to keep holding on.

As parents and educators, it is very important to be cognizant of enabling. Perhaps a child is not changing his ways because of our behavior. Therefore, let's take a good look at ourselves, assess the situation, and empower ourselves to help our children make positive changes in their lives.

After all, if we do not let them suffer the consequences of their actions, why should they change those actions? Usually, change comes about when one is hurting and wants to stop the hurt. Well, if you stop the hurt, if you make it all better, if you enable your child, then he does not have to do the changing. And, and this is a big and, if he doesn't do the changing, then he will learn nothing from the experience!

You know, often it is just easier for us, as parents, to do, but the easier way is not always the correct and constructive way. To enable or not to enable…the choice is ours, but the results are vastly different.

***

An Old Pair of Shoes

The other day I was putting on an old pair of shoes…and I thought to myself, "These are so soothing, so comfortable. They're just like an old friend."

Old friends are really special; they make you feel good. You have chosen to be with them. They "wear" easily.

With old shoes and old friends, you are able to walk through rough spots and survive. A matter of fact, with old friends, the bumps and bruises we meet along the way actually make your friendship stronger. They allow us to share more and to solve problems together, learning more about each other in the process.

Every once in a while, you may stop to polish your shoes. In like manner, every once in a while it's important to look with fresh eyes at your friendship and to smooth over any rough edges.

With shoes, it is important not to lace them too tightly. You need to give your feet space to breathe and to feel comfortable. With a friend, too, it is important not to crowd him; rather, you should give him some space. Let him be his own person. Let him feel free to voice his own thoughts. Smothering will make him uncomfortable and harm your friendship.

With shoes and a good friend, you can put them away for a while. Yet when you take them out, they are still comfortable. Yes, isn't it amazing? You may not speak to a good friend for a long time, but when you do, you are able to pick up where you left off. The comfortable feeling exists. The relationship is as strong as always.

Most importantly, both shoes and friends must give you a good foundation; they both must give you support. In this way, you will be able to be yourself and know that your friend will be there for you to pick you up when you are down and to applaud your successes when you are up.

So do choose to keep those old friends; just like your old pair of shoes, they are there when you need them and make you feel so good.

***

Ownership

I decided I had it. I had been working with Paul for weeks, hoping his grades would rise, hoping he would get his act together and stay out of trouble, hoping so many things, but to no avail. My wit's end came when warnings arrived and true to form, Paul earned the distinction of receiving them in all his major subjects. And to make matters worse, I had received three behavior slips from the Vice Principal. All the talks Paul and I had certainly didn't sink in. Now what...?

I called Paul into my office. He gave me his usual big smile, sat down at my desk and waited for me to begin. I mentioned his warnings.

He thought for a minute, didn't look too upset, and said, "Well, you know, I have to work after school. Then, when I do get home, there's a lot of confusion in my house, so I can't concentrate and I do have to help my folks with some chores."

"Oh," I said, "you've given me some excuses for the warnings, but what are the reasons? You're the one who is in control of what you wish to do. If work is interfering with your studying, then cut down your hours. If your brothers and sisters make too much noise, find another place to study. But, Paul, don't blame outside happenings for your problems!"

"But Mrs. Cohen," he countered, "you have no idea what it's like. How do you expect me to find another place to study? And what would my boss say if I asked to have my hours cut? Oh, and I need the money for my car payments."

We bantered back and forth and what came out loud and clear was that Paul had no intention of taking ownership of his actions. His grades, in his mind, were not his fault. Hey, it's always easier that way. Blame someone else. That kind of lets you off the hook.

From grades, we went on to his acting out and of course, he felt his getting written up wasn't his fault. The teachers just didn't like him. Yes, this kid just wasn't taking ownership of his actions, and without taking ownership, the problems really weren't problems that he caused so why should he be the one who should have to fix them?

I asked him if he knew the story of the *Three Little Pigs*. Of course, he looked at me like I was crazy, but he did recount the story and what he came to realize was that the pigs had to blame themselves for having their houses blown down. They had to take ownership of the fact that they had not built their houses of sturdy materials that would withstand the huffs from the mean old wolf. The one who wisely used brick still had his home.

We discussed other instances of ownership. If he didn't check the oil in his car and the engine seized, whose fault was that? On the football field, if he fumbled the ball and the other team recovered, whose fault was that? Next time, would he continue to fumble, or would he take ownership of the fact that he messed up and then decide to change?

"Well," I continued, looking him squarely in the eye, "I hate to tell you this, Paul, but the grades and your actions do belong to you. And because they do belong to you, only you can change them. Only you can decide you own them and only you can make them better. So, my friend, the ball's in your hands. Now it's your decision if you want to keep fumbling or not. The choice is yours."

Well, Paul did not change overnight. Things just don't happen that way. But gradually, he started to improve. He kept a list of all the test grades, saw what he was earning and took ownership of those grades. And that was the big step…ownership.

***

Part of the Problem or Part of the Solution?

So many times situations occur; we try to handle them in an appropriate fashion, but do we? Do we really stop and look at how we deal with the problem and ascertain whether we are part of the problem or part of the solution? Too many times, if we actually did some truthful searching, I think we would find that we have chosen to be part of the problem. Think about some of these examples.

Mrs. Jones comes into school. Sara is not doing well; her grades are poor, she doesn't come to school, and success does not seem to be in the picture. I ask Mrs. Jones what she has tried to do. She tells me that she has threatened to ground Sara, give her an earlier curfew, and take away her car.

"Have you followed through on these threats, or are they just that, threats?"

Mrs. Jones thinks for a moment and then has to admit that she has not followed through. She keeps thinking things will improve and keeps giving second and third chances. Who knows what chance she is up to now? In her mind, she is being a good parent, but the question is, is she really helping her child? Is she making her see that there will be consequences for her actions? In truth, the answer to all these questions is a resounding, "No"!! Instead, she is enabling the situation to continue and in so doing, she is part of the problem.

Another scenario… Poor Jimmy, his life has been so difficult; he really seems to have no goals and often slacks off in his schoolwork. Now that Grandma has come to town, she sees to it that all his wants are met. New clothes are bought, he is given a car to use, and he is showered with other gifts as well. But you know what, by being so good, by giving him the tangibles, Grandma is contributing to the problem of Jimmy's aimlessness.

Instead, she should be encouraging him to get a job. Perhaps she can tell him to put half his earnings in the bank and she will match them. Yet, by giving Jimmy so much, has she taught him responsibility? Has she taught him to fend for himself? Perhaps Grandma should sit down with him and talk to him. Together, they can write down some goals and then decide how Jimmy will achieve them. Will giving him a car help him to be focused on his schoolwork? I don't think so. Giving, giving, giving is okay, as long as some receiving is done, too.

What about Kelly? She is always late for school; however, when her parents are called, Mom is forever making excuses for her. Either the car wouldn't start or the alarm did not go off on time. Clearly, it is never Kelly's fault. But what has Mom done? She has not helped Kelly take responsibility for her actions. Instead, she has become part of the problem and has allowed the tardiness to continue and even to increase. Hey, if someone does not hurt, if someone is not made to feel uncomfortable, why should she change?

Really, it's okay for your child to feel uncomfortable, to even fail sometimes or to suffer some consequences for inappropriate actions. Only in this way will he grow. Only in this way will he learn. Only in this way will he be accountable for his actions and yes, only in this way will he begin to feel really good about his positive actions, because he – not you –has earned them.

So next time a situation arises, or perhaps there is an existing one that needs dealing with, do some real soul searching and ask yourself the following very important question, "Am I part of the problem or am I part of the solution?" Then, make a conscious effort to choose to become part of the solution.

***

I feel ...because...why?

Wow! That title may sound a little weird, but trust me, it is loaded with important stuff. Let me explain.

Poor Nancy. She has felt a little down. Her parents are separated and getting a divorce and her grandmother has recently died. To say she has a lot on her mind is an understatement. She is confused and upset. Concentration is out of the question.

"Nancy, I want you to keep a journal of your thoughts. You know, put down on paper how you feel. Then, you can look at what you have written and deal with it."

Looking at me, Nancy retorted, "Mrs. Cohen, I couldn't possibly do that! Like I couldn't even think what to write! What's the point anyway? What's happened has happened."

Looking at her, I responded, "The point is, Nancy, that you don't know what to write because you have not allowed yourself to really consider the issues. It's too painful to really think things through and unless you allow yourself to do that you will not be able to deal with the problems in your life. You know, some of the issues cannot be changed; you don't have the power to do that. You know, as hard as you may try, Mom and Dad are probably never going to get back together again, but you can change how you feel about it and how you plan to deal with those feelings. Do you understand what I am getting at?"

And so our conversation continued. Finally, I gave Nancy an assignment. I told her that I wanted her to take a piece of paper and to write the following on it. When I think of my mother, I feel...and then answer because and why you feel that way.

I said, "Do some serious thinking. Get it down on paper, bring it back to me tomorrow and then we will discuss it. I want you to go through the same routine for your dad and for your sister and brother. This is not an easy assignment, Nancy, but it will help you to look at some of the things in your life that are troubling and then to deal with them. Actually, you can use this exercise for other things and other people, too. For instance, when you think about school, you feel...because... why..."

So many times we are confronted with issues. We are upset, but we choose to not really address why we are upset. Instead, our being upset is kept inside of us where it turns into depression. The depression stops us in our tracks. We sit and dwell…not necessarily on the issues that have caused us to be unhappy, but rather on the fact that we are feeling down.

We wallow in self-pity. We feel no one can help us. We may become anxious. How will we get through the day? Nothing will improve.

Yes, you are probably right. Things won't improve until you stop letting the issues own you and you start to own them; you have to start to do something about them. Write them down, look at them, and begin to deal with them.

Now you get my drift. The title of this does make sense. Instead of being anxious, confused and seemingly finding no solutions, you will see that your problems will become clearer and more manageable if you complete the following – I feel…because… why. You will have focus and from this focus will come insight.

***

Plom

This is not a typo, nor is it an exotic type of fruit. It's an acronym for Poor Little Ole Me…and you'd be surprised to learn how many people suffer from it!

Lynne came to see me just the other day. Actually, I had called her in because she was not performing as well as she had previously and I wanted to find out if there could be an underlying reason for this.

She pulled up a chair, looked at me, and smiled when I asked, "Is there something I should know about that's going on in your life? Could there be anything that's filling your mind and not leaving room for studying?"

She pondered this for a moment and then proceeded to list a number of things that were in fact troubling her. She and her boyfriend had decided to call it quits. Although it was a mutual decision, it was still hurtful. Her dog, whom she had for fourteen years, had died. Then, too, her mom and dad were getting a divorce. Actually Dad had moved out and she was living with Mom. Mom has been upset and it has been difficult for Lynne to have any type of communications with her.

Lynne continued by saying, "You know, Mrs. Cohen, I really don't care about my classes, and to tell you the truth, I have trouble paying attention and often fall asleep. Why should I care anyway? Life really stinks."

Lynne was suffering from PLOM and choosing to have a pity party.

After listening to Lynne's tale of woe, I told her that it's obvious she has a lot on her mind. Actually, she has had a lot of losses and has not worked them out. In the past, she has talked to Mom, but now Mom has her own issues and is not really available for long discussions.

With Lynne's assistance, I wrote down all of her losses so she could actually look at them. I added to the list grades, since it was evident that she no longer was winning in that department. Then, we proceeded to look at each loss and determine what could be done.

Grades could be worked on. Extra help could be sought, friends could be called, teachers could be seen after school and more studying could be done. However, none of that could or would take place until some of the other issues were worked through.

She talked to me about her dog. Yes, it hurt that Rusty was not in her life, yet she realized that he had gotten old and frail and had been suffering. Perhaps she could get a new dog. If not, she could gain comfort from realizing that she had spent quality time with him and he with her. There were memories and she could never be robbed of those.

Next, we looked at her breakup with Tim. After sharing some facts and feelings with me, she realized that the relationship had to end. It was doing neither one of them any good. However, she also realized that she had learned from the relationship, so although she felt sad that it was over, she came to realize it was time to move on.

Then, we tackled the "biggy"...Mom and Dad. Ah...that was a big problem. I mean that was one Lynne could not fix. She had to become accepting of the fact that her parents were getting a divorce, yet she had to be able to separate their actions from themselves as people. They still loved her; she still loved them. Their actions, though she did not like them, were separate from her. She had to internalize that and deal with it.

As we talked further, Lynne told me that she would sleep for many hours. Often she would go to sleep as soon as she got home in the afternoon.

"Tell me why you think you sleep so much," I asked.

Lynne had no clue; she just felt it was because she was so tired. Instead, I suggested that she slept to escape her problems, to forget about her losses. Also, she has tired herself out from wallowing in self-pity.

"The only problem is, Lynne, that when you awaken the problems are still there. You can't avoid them. You can't hide from them. So face them. Change the ones that you can. Accept the issues that cannot be changed. It won't be easy, but it's the only thing that will bring you relief and allow you to become productive again."

I continued, "You know, Lynne, it would be good to use some of your energies in a positive way. Avoid making excuses. Avoid the PLOM syndrome."

While she looked quizzically at me I explained, "PLOM…poor little ole me. You can choose to continue to wear that badge and be stuck, or you can take it off, deal with your losses, and move on."

What will Lynne choose? I have no idea. But I do hope that she really listened and will start making some changes. Only she can shake the PLOM and start moving forward with her life.

***

Forgiveness

It's incredible how so many people let their past continue to consume them and own them! I was talking to a grown man the other day who still harbors ill feelings towards his parents, one of whom is no longer even living!

I said to him, "I can't believe it, you are letting the man own you even from the grave!"

As he continued to speak to me, I could hear and feel his anger. It was governing the way he was acting and talking. Wasn't it time for this man to get on with his life? Wasn't it time for him to choose to let go?

What to do? Well, for starters, I think it's time to practice forgiveness. Actually, Dave has two choices. He can either stay angry, or give it up and let himself be free. It's time he realized that there is another way to deal with his pain;

obviously the way he has been dealing with it is self-defeating; it doesn't feel good; it is stultifying and will not allow him to grow.

But it is hard to practice forgiveness. Why? It's because you have to choose to dig in and let surface those feelings that you have buried inside, those feelings that you buried alive because you were not able to deal with them. Up until now, you have not truly looked for nurture, comfort or support. You have distanced yourself from others because you don't want to have to open up. When you find others are getting too close to you, you become panicked, you feel oppressed, and you start to turn those people away. After all, you have been hurt by others who have been close to you and you don't want to experience any more pain. You do not have room for it. Many times, you just try to stop feeling!

But it doesn't work because you are carrying all this baggage, this resentment, and it is weighing you down especially at night when you find you can't sleep. Subconsciously, those feelings are trying to speak out; you're trying to suppress them, and that isn't conducive to sleep.

You know, forgiveness really doesn't have anything to do with the other person; it has everything to do with you. You must choose to make a conscious decision to have a good life, to be whole again. When you use your past experiences as excuses to your problems, you are letting the experiences, not you, take responsibility for your life and your actions. If you continue to nurture your hurts, if you continue to carry them around, they will continue to stifle you, to hinder you from moving along with your life. And actually, you will start to feel isolated because people will not want to be around you; they will sense your anger and your depression and will not want to share it.

Do you realize how much energy it takes to keep the hurt alive? By doing this, you are taking vital energy away from you that could be used for positive things. By continually blaming, you will be living in the past and not taking charge of the present.

You need to start healing yourself. You need to tell yourself that the person who caused you all this pain was doing the best that he could do at the time. Because of his nurturing, relationships, parenting, etc., he reacted to you in a certain manner and that was the best he could do. Now, you must forgive him to go on. What he did was not okay. But you must let go of the intense emotions, of the anger surrounding what he did, telling yourself that you have better things to do with your life.

Do talk to the person who caused you pain. What he did was not right, but by forgiving him, you are letting go and allowing yourself to live. So choose to let go of the anger. It is depleting you. When you do this, you will find peace in your life. Anger will no longer be holding you hostage. Once you have chosen forgiveness, you will be free, free to be the person that you are so capable of becoming.

***

Life Is Not A Video

Today I had a young man in my office. Clearly distraught, he was making a move into our school and really did not want to do this. However, family issues were such that a move was not only inevitable, but also warranted.

Sitting across from me, he was forlorn, but more than that, he was angry. How dare adults decide his life! How dare adults take away his pleasure of connecting with his friends! How dare adults bring such misery on him! And so the "pity party" continued. I let him talk; it was good for him to vent. I knew eventually he would stop and I would get my chance. Then it came. Silence.

"Well, Jim," I said, " I hear that you are upset. Life is not always fair. It is hard. But you have choices. You can either wallow in self-pity, or move along and make the best of a situation."

Then the thought hit me; life is not a video. I asked Jim if he watched videos. Like duh…of course he did.

"You know, sometimes I wish life were like a video, but it's not and you know why? With a video you can hit different buttons and make things happen. You can hit the pause button, the rewind button, the fast forward button, and even the menu button – if you have a DVD- and this will allow you to visit certain scenes and do many other things. But with life you just can't do that."

Then, I went on to elaborate exactly what I meant. Jim interjected his thoughts and listened intently, too. After all, he could relate to videos and this was his life we were discussing!

Let's take a look at some of my points. Unlike a video, our life is animate and continuous while we are here on this earth. We cannot push a stop button and halt everything. Inexorably, life continues on its way. Day becomes night and night becomes day. We cannot push a pause button. Sometimes we would like to just pause everything, maybe because we are truly enjoying what we are doing and wish we could experience it for a longer period of time. Maybe we are afraid of moving on and just wish we could stay where we are; however, pausing indefinitely is not possible. Life goes forward and we with it.

And what about the rewind button? Can't we go back to where we were and forget about all of the stuff that is happening now? Not possible. Can we revisit scenes in our life? Yes, but we can revisit them only in our minds, not in reality. Again, we must continue to move forward. Yet, we cannot push fast forward. We must live each day and then go onto the next. It is impossible to skip over Monday, Tuesday, and Wednesday and then stop on Thursday.

And then I said to Jim, "So you see, life is a continuum; we cannot stop it. What we can do is close the door on the past, knowing we can never reclaim it. We move on. Sure we can use our memory to revisit things and maybe we can slow down our pace a bit, but the truth is we do move on. We move on knowing that we cannot rewind our life. For us humans, the camera keeps recording. We have to embrace the here and now, do the best we can with it, and then look forward to tomorrow. Jim, you cannot change what was, you cannot stop where you are, but you can start where you are, realizing that this is your life and you can choose to either make the most of it or not; the choice is yours. One thing that is clear is that it will continue no matter how you choose to view it."

***

This was written in response to the pain of a young person who had to choose to shed the shackles of his past in order to get on with his life.

The Octopus and the Young Man

The octopus hung on tightly
His eight arms were squeezing
Squeezing, squeezing
Squeezing the essence
Out of the young man's body
Breathing was labored
Thinking was obfuscated
The octopus was winning
It was in control
The arms of parenting

Judy Cohen

The arms of childhood
The arms of bitter emotions
All were encompassing the young man
And suffocating him
His eyes were glazed…
Darkness was closing in
The pain became unbearable
Something had to be done
Slowly the young man started stirring
Slowly he started to twist
Then in earnest he pulled
With every fiber of his being
The right to exist was powerful
It led him forward
He lashed out at his predator
He cut off one arm, then another
Slowly the chains gave way
The octopus, holding onto the past
Holding onto the traumas
Started to retreat
Oxygen flowed to the young man's brain
Thought processes renewed
The past was being shed
The chains were being broken
The young man's essence was being restored
There was a final powerful push…
The octopus relinquished his prey
Wounded, he slowly crawled away
The young man watched him go
Hope started to fill his lungs
Gulps of fresh air were inhaled
His eyesight became keener
The grayness rescinded
He was now free…
Free to be, free to explore, free to exist
Without the shackles of the octopus

***

Who is Defining Whom?

I was at a meeting the other day and heard an interesting sentence that really stuck with me.

The speaker said, "Do not let others define you; choose to define yourself."

How essential it is for all of us to consider that sentence, especially for our youngsters today who are so concerned with what others think about their every move. I cannot begin to count the number of times that a youngster has come into my office with tears streaming down her face because she doesn't feel included or liked, simply because the others in the group don't like the ideas that she espouses.

She begins to wonder if her ethic, if the fiber of her being is wrong. Should she choose to be more like some of her peers and abandon her beliefs, in order to be accepted? This is a tough question, since a yes answer means she will be included and a no answer means she will be excluded. With this particular gal, we sat and chatted about the situation.

"First of all," I inquired, " just who are you, Heidi? What makes you tick? What do you like to do, what do you believe?" I emphasized the word you each time I spoke.

Once we had looked more closely at the real Heidi, we then tackled the same questions and came up with answers that would fit the "group". We compared and contrasted the two sets of answers and you guessed it...the answers were different. Next, we tackled what Heidi really wanted. Did she want to change her way of thinking and let the group's way define her, or did she want to hold steadfastly to her own ideals? Was she willing to redefine herself to fit the group's image to belong, or was it time for her to hang up the idea of belonging to that group and instead seek friends who shared her way of thinking and acting? The group's way of thinking and acting was not necessarily wrong, but was it right for Heidi and that's what she had to consider.

I think intellectually she knew what she had to do, but emotionally she was torn because she so wanted to hang with that group. She felt caught between who she was and who she wished she could be. But the question was, did she want the group to define her, or did she want to define herself? In Heidi's case, I am glad she grappled with the issues and decided to be herself, the Heidi that she knew.

Let's think for a moment how many times we do let things define us. The advertisements on television certainly leave their mark. Often, we purchase items that we never would have bought before. The commercials have, in fact, helped to define us. What about the movies and television programs? Many times, youngsters will try to pattern themselves after one of the stars. Now, who is defining whom?

As adults, our slates are pretty much filled with ideas, thoughts, and actions. We are pretty much defined. Yet, as a child, slates are still being written upon. Unless a child has a good sense of self, he will often let additional ideas be imprinted on his slate that perhaps should not be there. The one who is surer of himself will be more selective in choosing what to allow on his slate.

When new situations arise, when we are exposed to different ways of thinking, it is good to take a deep look at ourselves and ask, "Do I wish to be defined by that, or do I choose to do my own defining?"

After all, the word define, according to Webster, means to determine the essential qualities of... It is good to know and embrace our essential qualities. They are the ones that make us uniquely us.

***

Blame

What a simple five letter word, but what a difference it can make in a person's life. I know it enters so many of the conversations that I have with my students. At times, I am really tempted to ask Webster to eliminate it from the dictionary!!!!

Sally enters my office. I have called her down to discuss her grades that are rapidly falling.

Sitting across from me, she meets my questioning gaze and responds, "You know, how can I possibly study? My brothers and sisters make so much noise. My mom wants me to do a lot of chores around the house, and you know I do have my sports that I play."

"Ah", I say, thinking well here's another one to put in the blame category. "You certainly have reasons for your poor grades, don't you, but I think you're overlooking another reason, another person."

I pause, hoping she'll catch my drift and single out that other person. After a minute or two of silence that I could have cut with a knife, I finally become a little more directive, actually downright directive, and say, "Haven't you forgotten to place yourself in this? You're the person whom you left out!"

Looking at me quizzically, Sally counters, "What do you mean?"

I proceed to tell her about the little five letter word BLAME.

"Sally, do you know the meaning of the word blame? It means to place responsibility on someone else. You know, it is so much easier to pick out someone else to blame for your problems instead of actually looking within yourself and owning the situation."

We talked about the objects of her blame. Yes, her brothers and sisters are noisy, but Sally could choose to go to the library to study. She could choose to not study in the den and instead go into her bedroom and close the door. Perhaps she could choose to study at a friend's. By pointing these options out to her, she could see that she was in control of choosing where to study. The situation would be the same, the noise would be there, but she would be able to circumvent the problem and study.

Concerning chores around the house, I told her to make a schedule and to place the chores on the schedule, leaving enough time to do her studying. Again, by making a schedule, she could control the outcome and accomplish her studying. When we looked at the chores together, she had to agree with me that they were not all that time consuming. The problem was that she was leaving them until the last minute or at times she was spending too much time dawdling and not getting them done or feeling so sorry for herself and stewing about them, that she was unable to accomplish anything!

I told her to use the same schedule to write down her sports practices and games. Then, she could readily see how she had to balance everything. Time management had to be learned and followed.

"You know, Sally," I continued after we had discussed scheduling, " when you spend your time blaming others, you are doing just that…spending time…and that time could and should be spent looking at the problems and coming up with solutions. Blaming sort of stops you in your tracks. It gets you stuck in the mud. Instead, choose to give yourself a push, look squarely within yourself and see what YOU can do to make things better."

It is so important for each of us to choose to do something about a problem; otherwise, we divorce ourselves from it and wait for those we are blaming to come up with solutions. Yet, if those we are blaming are not truly the cause of the problem, then how can they truly provide the solution? Blaming is paralyzing; solution making is action producing.

***

Attitude

One small word, but what a difference it makes. Attitude really does control our lives. Different things may beset us, things we may not have any control over, but then it's how we choose to think about those happenings and ultimately deal with them that determine our happiness or despair, our success, or our failure.

Dave came into my office yesterday. Clearly he was very upset. His teacher, he felt, was being unfair to him. Each day became harder and harder for him to bear her seemingly unjust barbs. Instead of confronting the teacher, instead of airing his thoughts, Dave decided to shut down.

He became angrier and angrier and decided, "I will get back at her. I just won't do anything. I don't care about her lousy homework and those awful tests."

So what happened? Dave's grades plummeted. Now he was close to failing the course. He internalized the failing grade and blamed the teacher for it. After all, it was the teacher who got him so annoyed, who made him stop caring and trying…or was it?

Poor Dave…I guess he was looking for my sympathy and understanding; however, that is not what I doled out.

"Dave, wait a minute," I countered, "Who took those tests? Who decided not to do his homework? Who decided to get so upset and seek revenge?"

Slowly Dave came to realize that he had to take ownership of his grade; he was the one who chose to respond to the teacher in the manner that he did. He was the one who copped the attitude and therefore had to live with the consequences.

Let's look at another scenario. What about the boss who takes on "a holier than thou" attitude? How does this impact his employees? Do they feel free to come to him with concerns? Do they produce more for him? Do they put in that little bit of extra time? I bet they don't. There's the old cliché, "You can catch a bee with honey" and how true it is. The nicer you treat someone, the nicer you, too, will be treated. Display a good attitude and those around you will mirror what they see.

What about the parent who is always complaining, who feels stuck, who wears a dour countenance, who mopes around the house and yells and finds fault? I will wager a bet that his children will develop a similar attitude. They, too, will mope around. The world will be colored in somber hues, not in sunny tones. Why? Because attitudes are catchy and because children are often reflections of whom they see.

What about the kid with the positive attitude…the one who says and thinks, "I can do it," the one who takes life as he finds it and deals with it? This is the kid who will succeed. This is the kid who will not make excuses, who will not blame others, who will look squarely at his issues and deal with them.

I still remember Kathy who was a special ed student. She was determined to make the grade. She applied herself diligently. She welcomed challenges, sought help, and kept a positive attitude. And you know what? She not only succeeded, she excelled and went on to a four-year college.

We don't really have control over life's forces. But we do have control over our attitudes. We can choose to greet the day with a smile or greet the day with a frown. We can choose to see the glass as half full, or we can look at the same glass and see it as half empty. That does enable us to be able to grapple with whatever may come our way. But will we grapple with those issues positively or negatively? Clearly the choice is ours and that choice will make all the difference.

***

Shoot for the Goal

Sean walked into my office. Actually, it was not on a voluntary basis; he was summoned. I had reached the breaking point. When the fourth teacher came to see me about Sean's skipping classes, I knew I had to take action. So, I decided to have a "heart-to-heart" with my client.

Visibly squirming in his seat, Sean was not a happy camper as I began to share what his teachers had told me.

Looking at me, he stopped fidgeting for a minute and replied, "I don't know. I guess I just don't like school".

Not skipping a beat, I looked him squarely in the eyes and responded, "That's a cop-out and you know it. You don't come to school, you choose to skip, you haven't performed well on your tests and when you do go to class, the teachers tell me that you don't pay attention. By the way, do you play a sport?"

Seemingly relieved that the conversation had seemed to take a turn and landed on safer ground, he eagerly answered the question. "Yes, I play soccer; I'm a forward."

"Ah, really, and just how do you prepare for your games?"

"Well, we meet with the coach; he outlines the plays. We listen, we practice them and then we use those plays on the field."

"Really?" I responded somewhat incredulously. "How is it that with the coach you listen, you practice and you perform, yet in the classroom you are unable to do any of those things? If you can do them in one arena, you can do them in another. By the way, what is the purpose of your doing the plays?"

I'm sure he thought I was now clearly out of my mind to ask such an easy question, but to his credit, he answered me by telling me he was a forward and would dribble the ball and then try to score by making a goal.

" Ah," I said, "I thought so, just checking. Do you think if you had a goal as far as school were concerned that you would listen, work hard, and perform in order to make the goal happen? Do you think you would decide to attend classes, just like you obviously have decided to attend practices?"

Sean got my meaning. We started talking about post high school plans and how to make them realities. Sean knew he had to come to school and do well in order to succeed. By skipping, he was accomplishing nothing positive. Sean now realizes that it is he who is in control of what he chooses to do. To shoot for the goal and graduate or not...clearly the choice is his.

***

Some Liquid for Thought

I know, I know, it's supposed to be food for thought, but forgive me, I took some poetic license. You see, I saw this quotation that I really like that I wish to share with you and comment on.

"People are like tea bags. They don't know their own strength until they get into hot water."

Think about that quotation. It rings true in just about every facet of life. When you think about sports, conjure up yourself or one of your children on the baseball diamond. There are two outs. Bases are loaded and you or your child is up to bat. What to do? Do you pull the ball, do you go for a homer, do you hit away? What kind of pitch will you receive? Yup, you're in hot water, but you don't fold; you focus, rise to the occasion, and wonders of wonders, your hit wins the game!

Let's take a look at Joan. She is forlorn. Not doing well in her subjects, she enters my office looking very dejected. Why should she even bother? Where should she even begin? It would be so much easier, she thinks, to just give up, let everything slide, fail and begin again in the fall. Right? No, wrong. As I explain to Joan, now is the time to really show her mettle. When the going gets tough, the tough get going and decide to really dig in.

Well, Joan and I sit together, discuss ways to deal with her seemingly overwhelming problem, and map out a plan. As the weeks ensue, and Joan works harder, she begins to see improvement. This gives her the impetus to work even harder and do even better. Right now, all her grades are up and we are both hopeful that she will pass the year.

What about the youngster who cheats on a test? The teacher catches him, rips up the exam, and rightfully gives the kid a zero. Clearly, the student is in hot water. What to do? Naturally, I hear about the happening from the teacher. I call Stanley in. He is agitated, hates the teacher and yells that things are unfair. Once I get him to calm down, I make him see the error of his ways and take ownership of the problem. He is the one who cheated. He is the one who caused his own misfortune. Together, we talk to the teacher. Stanley apologizes. In his case, he is lucky; the teacher accepts the apology and lets Stan do some other work for some credit. From the hot water he had gotten into, Stan has learned some important lessons. Honesty is the best policy; one needs to take ownership of his mistakes; one has to show strength of character and apologize.

I still remember when Matt got into hot water. He applied to colleges without really discussing with his parents what they could afford. Well, you guessed it. He was accepted to the schools, but the financial aid packages he received did not make attending the schools a possibility. Or did they? Matt talked to me. He was in hot water. What could he do? He wanted to go to one of these schools. Since his parents did not have the resources to help him, we considered other options. Matt decided he could work during the summer, do two jobs, and earn enough money for one year. Then, he would take on the next year.

I heard from him at the end of the summer. Clearly, he sounded exhausted, but excited as well. He had done it! He could finance his first year, and with work-study and an additional job, he would have enough spending money for books and other expenses. He shared with me that initially he thought he could never make it happen, yet through adversity, he developed strength and renewed focus.

All of these happenings took place because people found themselves in hot water. Yet undaunted, people found inner strength to change their situation, to make unfortunate circumstances into positive ones. If they had not been tested through adversity, they never would have realized what they were capable of accomplishing.

***

To Lie or Not to Lie, That is the Question

The other day Beth came into my office. I had called her in as I do all of my students, just to talk, to get a handle on the person, and to find out if everything is going okay. Actually, even before I got around to calling Beth in, her mom had called me, had expressed some concerns and wondered if I could speak to her.

Well, Beth came in and took a seat. A nice looking and very personable young gal, Beth readily looked me in the eye and spoke directly to me. I started with some pleasantries and then, not wanting to hide anything from her, I told her that her mom had called.

Immediately, I noticed a change in her demeanor. Her eyes were downcast, a dour look came over her face, and she retorted with a sharp, "Yeah? What did SHE want?"

Beth proceeded to tell me that things were not great at home. Her parents did not seem to trust her; they would always question her about where she was going, with whom, and then sometimes even make phone calls to find out if she were really at so and so's house. And that really burned her!

"Beth," I asked. "Why do you think they don't trust you? Have you ever done anything that would cause that to happen?"

She thought for a moment and then began to share some things with me. It seems that she figured out a while back that when she would tell the truth it would come back to haunt her. She would be punished if she said that she had come home at 10 instead of at 9 or that she really cleaned up her room when, in fact, her sister had picked things up. And these were just some of the examples.

Each time she would be yelled at and consequences would follow. So, she figured, why should she tell the truth? The less her parents knew, the better. Why tell them things that would get them angry, so Beth got used to telling "little white lies". She would just change the truth a little. In that way, she would not get into trouble. And the more she lied and didn't get caught, the more she would continue to lie. It became easier not to tell the truth.

Well, you guessed it. One day, changing the truth to serve her needs came back to hurt her. Mom had shown up at school to drop something off for her and had bumped into one of her teachers who informed Mom that Beth had been slacking off and was not doing well in her class. The teacher was concerned. She had sent a note home, but had never heard from Mom. Of course Mom had never received the note. After all, Beth was afraid of reprisals and figured she would be able to recoup her grade and no one would be the wiser. She simply had told her folks that school was super, her grades were good, and all was fine.

Well, she and I talked about lying. We talked about how lying leads to not being trusted. Her parents couldn't trust her because they didn't know if what Beth was telling them she did was based on fact or fiction. What to do?

Clearly, Beth had to mend her ways, but then, too, so did her parents. They had made things so difficult for Beth when she was truthful, that Beth had decided to lie to escape their wrath. So, a meeting was held with Beth and her parents.

Once everyone was in my office, I elicited from Beth that she had lied to her parents on occasion and then pushed her to tell them why. Her parents looked aghast. They seemed to have no idea that they had come down on her so hard and that by doing so they had forced her hand into lying. They felt all kids needed consequences when they had done something that was not right, so wasn't it fair that Beth be punished?

I explained to them that in theory I agreed with them, but punished is a harsh word. Discussion is a much better one. If they asked Beth to choose to be truthful, then shouldn't they reward that truthfulness with listening to her, giving her a chance to share her side, and coming up with a reasonable consequence for her actions?

In that way, they would be encouraging her to be honest, they would not be yelling at her, they would be telling her that her actions were not right and along with Beth, they would try to rectify the situation.

You know, we are all human beings; we all make mistakes. And that's okay, but we need to learn from our mistakes. We need to be able to discuss our mistakes, own up to them without fear of reprisals, and then conduct ourselves in a manner that will negate those mistakes from happening in the future.

To lie or not to lie...that's really not the question. To listen and help, that should be what one is concerned with. Then, to lie or not to lie would not even be a choice.

***

Depression, Grieving, Healing

Daylight Will Come

I still remember when Bill walked into my office. It was obvious that he was upset. His head was hanging down, he was wiping his eyes, and he asked if I had a tissue. All of this was done with his eyes averted from mine. As he fidgeted, I searched for a tissue and then invited him to sit down. He sort of plopped into the seat with a thud, and continued his downward gaze. Gently, I asked him to tell me how he was feeling, although it was pretty obvious.

Haltingly, he replied in a very quiet voice, "I don't know. Everything seems so black. I can't fall asleep at night; I can't get up in the morning. I can't concentrate and my grades are really bad! What's the matter with me?"

Upon further probing, I found out that his appetite is nil, he isn't interested in hanging with his friends, and nothing seems to excite him anymore. I told him that I thought he was suffering from depression and I would like to talk to his parents about it. He seemed very nervous, so I added that there are many reasons for depression and once the reason is known, appropriate treatment can be given.

"Daylight will come, Bill. This darkness will fade, and the sun will come out, but you have to bear with me, trust my suggestions, and discuss your feelings with your folks."

Well, Bill and I did talk to his folks who suggested he was probably tired. Clearly, their son could not have depression. I mean isn't that a mental illness? We went back and forth for a while. Finally, they agreed to take Bill to their family doctor.

Bill was diagnosed with depression, put on medication, and greatly improved. However, after a time, he did reappear in my office, clearly upset again. It seems he had been feeling so well that he took it upon himself to stop the medication and now he was clearly in a funk. Actually, it was a blessing in disguise. Now he clearly understood that he needed the medication.

"Bill, you should never feel ashamed that you are talking medication. If you were a diabetic, you would take insulin. Your body needs this to function correctly, so listen to your body and be good to it."

Bill resumed the medication and had to wait a few weeks for it to kick in. I am delighted to say that it did its magic again and Bill became a viable, happy, and productive member of our school's community. He has since graduated and gone to college where he is flourishing.

Please, parents and kids, be aware of depression. It can and does strike anyone. Depression is an illness. It is not willed; it is not imagined. Many times it is a chemical imbalance. With the proper treatment, the illness can be treated effectively. If you suspect depression, don't wait and think it will disappear by itself. Do contact a counselor and your doctor. With appropriate help, the blackness will disappear and daylight will come!

***

The Sun Will Shine

"May I come in? Is this a good time? Do you have as minute to talk?"

As I looked up from my desk, there stood Martha. A very bright girl with a usually cheerful demeanor, Martha now looked distraught. I beckoned her to come in and she sat down across from me.

"Pull the chair up a little closer", I suggested. I didn't want her to feel isolated.

Well, all I had to say was, "How are you?" and the dam broke.

Through her tears she told me that she has been unhappy and she just doesn't know why. Her head hurt, her stomach hurt, but she really didn't think she was sick. Yet, she would cry at the drop of a hat, have trouble sleeping, and her appetite was almost nonexistent.

I listened as she gave me her tale of woe and then asked her if she finds she is unusually tired, if she feels lost and bewildered and incapable of performing many tasks and if she is having trouble concentrating. She answered yes to most of my questions.

"You know, Martha, I really think you are depressed. Depression is nothing to be ashamed about; it is real. Sometimes it visits us for a little while; sometimes it stays for a long while. It's okay to feel down, but when that feeling interferes with your life over a period of time, then you are suffering from clinical depression. The good news is that there is help for you."

And so the conversation continued. Martha is not unique. Over the years I have had other students who have suffered from depression. Many sought out appropriate help and were able to go on with their lives in a productive manner.

Depression is marked by a sense of overwhelming sadness. The depressed person seems unable to move, often suffers from panic attacks and seems stuck. He is unable to get on with his life even though he may wish to do so. He may experience guilt, low self-esteem and a sense of futility. He may have many friends but thinks he has none. Sleep may come too frequently or not at all.

Many feel their depressive episodes are exacerbated by the gloominess of the winter weather in the North. Others seem to be negatively affected by working in dark places. This type of depression is called SAD…Seasonal Affective Disorder.

What causes people to be depressed? Sometimes it is caused by an underlying genetic link; most of the times it is caused by life experiences. Females seem to experience depression more than males.

What to do? Talking through your feelings may help; other times it is necessary to not only seek professional help through counseling, but also to take prescribed medications.

When a person experiences an inconsistency in his behavior, he may have Bipolar Disorder; he may cycle between highs (mania) and lows(depression). He lacks balance in his life; he seems to be one person for a certain length of time and then another person. It is upsetting to him and the rest of his family. Most times this condition begins in teenagers and young adults. It is difficult to diagnose, but once a professional diagnoses it, medication can be given and the sufferer can be helped to lead a good life.

If your child displays some of the symptoms of depression and they seem to last for an inordinate length of time, do seek help. Do not be ashamed; depression is an illness and like many illnesses it can be successfully treated, but only if you reach out for assistance. With treatment, the days will stop looking bleak and dreary and in time, the sun will shine.

***

Loss

It's amazing, but people usually only think you go through a feeling of loss when someone has died; however, any type of loss necessitates coming to grips with the situation. And it really does not matter if you are young or old; each must grieve the loss.

I find that people who are grieving go through different stages, although each stage is not clear-cut and does not necessarily have an exact ending. You may revisit a stage and deal with it again and again and then finally when you have dealt with it, you can move on.

Let's think of some losses…divorce, death, a breakup with a boyfriend or girlfriend, fired from a job, moving to a new location, loss of a limb, etc. Each one of the above causes change in one's life and this change causes pain that must be worked through. Each loss does cause grieving.

Initially, when someone hears about loss, there is a general numbness, a feeling that a bad dream is occurring and the grieving person will awaken from the nightmare to find all is okay. The person experiences a surreal feeling and starts to deny the actual happening of the loss. I think denial comes into play in order to let the body adjust a little bit to the idea of loss.

Next comes the idea of bargaining. "If onlies" are played over and over again. "Perhaps if I do such and such, the loss will be reversed." Daily living may become overwhelming.

At this point, anger often rears its ugly head. The grieving person is angry at the world, at a higher power, at the perpetrator of the loss. "Why me?" And then the blaming comes in because something or someone must have caused this loss, is responsible for it, and at least the grieving person can direct his negative energy toward that someone or something.

Often anger is followed by guilt. "I must be a really bad person for this to happen!" This is often played again and again in the grieving person's mind and actually makes the person enter the next stage that is depression.

The person is really exhausted at this point. Even when the sun shines, the whole world looks gray. Simple tasks become monumental to perform. Sleeping and eating may become erratic. Often, medical attention is sought.

But, just when the bereaved thinks the depression will never end, the real healing stage begins, and he starts to surrender to the idea that the loss has occurred. He starts to slowly involve himself in more social activities and not feel so isolated. The weight of the world has lessened and he is able to reach out to others and not be so self-involved. He is able to surrender his feelings and really start to come to grips with them.

Finally, acceptance of the loss arrives and he starts to rejoin the world of the living. He realizes he can make it. He can survive. He can go on and live and start immersing himself more in his studies, friend's hobbies, or whatever fits.

During the grieving process, it is important to talk to other people. Reach out to them and share your emotions. Do not let them bottle up. If you share feelings, you are giving the listener a chance to share, too. Often, others don't know what to say. By breaking the ice and voicing your thoughts, you give others license to communicate with you.

Each person who has experienced a loss needs to go through stages in order to come out whole. The process is painful, but it is the only way healing can occur. There will be good times and bad times. Feel the bad times, know they will pass; then embrace and cherish the good times. Soon, you will notice that the good times will occur more frequently than the bad times. Do reach out, enable yourself to heal, and embrace life, since life is for the living.

***

Why?

Unfortunately, our high school has lost several students over the years to untimely deaths. Students ponder and adults ponder the question why? Why were they taken from our midst?

Yes, that's the question on the minds of so many. And as the distraught students enter my office tearfully and pose that question, I have to look at them and say, "There is no answer. I am truly sorry."

Then, with tears brimming in their eyes, I ask each one to tell me about the deceased. Sharing helps. Keeping her memory alive helps. I tell them to write memories down or perhaps make a collage. We talk about the stages they have gone through, what they are going through and what will probably ensue. I encourage them to feel. Feelings will be different for different people. There is no right or wrong way to grieve, but it is important to let their feelings surface.

Now many are on "automatic pilot"; they function as usual and just feel that this whole thing didn't happen. They may be overcome with numbness or a sense of denial. Actually, this is nature's way of giving their bodies a chance to adjust until they are ready to deal with the reality of death.

Some teens become very angry and that's okay. Anger allows them to vent their emotions. So does crying…tears are healing.

Some teens feel guilt. They play the "if only" game. Maybe if they had been with the person, this would not happen. They may remember when they had had an argument with the deceased and now feel guilty that they did. It is important that they know that this is a natural way to feel.

Some teens will turn to drugs/alcohol to lessen their pain of grieving. Actually, although they may temporarily numb the pain, they, in fact, may prolong and complicate the grieving process. As parents, be on the lookout for your teenager's attempt to self –medicate.

What can you as parents do to help your teenagers? The best thing is to listen. Ask them to share with you stories of the person who has died. Perhaps they have a picture of the person. Don't avoid the subject of death. Don't try to change the subject. If you do, you will be closing off any discussion and making your teenagers feel isolated. In addition, they may sense that it is not right to feel and will begin to hide their feelings from you.

Do not try to fix their pain. You can't. Only time, talking, and final acceptance can do that. Be open to their questions, but be honest, too. When they ask why don't be afraid to tell them that sometimes there just are no answers.

Some students wonder why they should continue to strive to do well; after all, one day they will die. Now they realize that death will come one day. They have seen it happen. What should you, as a parent, do? I have found that it works to listen, but then to advise.

"You know, we all die, but we all are born, too. We don't know exactly when someone will be born and we don't know when someone will die. But we do know that we can grasp what is in between and live life to its fullest. We do have the power to do that."

Finally letting go of their grief doesn't mean forgetting. It means being able to go on with one's life .If your teenagers' grieving process seems prolonged, if sleeplessness continues, if bad dreams continue, if their appetite is lessened, if concentration seems to become more difficult and grades seem to be suffering, then you, as a parent, should step in and make an appointment for them to seek the services of a professional.

The most important message I have for you, parents, is just to be there…be there to comfort, to share, and most of all to love and to listen.

***

Feeling is Healing

I still can see Becky when she came into my office. I knew tragedy had struck in her family, so I had called her in to see how she was coping. She walked into my office, sat in a chair, looked squarely at me when she spoke, and answered my simple questions clearly, yet succinctly. Frankly, my first impression was that she was "all together" and doing O.K. Then, I probed a little further, asked more detailed questions and got closer to the issue of feeling.

Right away, I perceived a difference in her attitude. She seemed to start to shut me out. She looked down at her hands, she wiggled in her seat and her voice became lower as she spoke. Clearly, she appeared agitated. It became apparent that Becky had done what so many do when they are hurting…she shut off her feelings in order to cope. Yet, had that really helped her to cope? If so, then why was she agitated?

In truth, unless one deals with feeling, there really is no healing. As with a physical wound, until we tend to it, it will continue to fester. Yes, we can Band-Aid it, but once that is removed, the wound will still be there. Instead, we must administer directly to the wound in order to have it heal.

Unfortunately, the wound may hurt a little more when the medicine is applied, but only in that way will it get cleansed and then eventually close. There's the old cliché, "No pain, no gain," and with feeling and healing, the cliché is so true. Becky had to really take her pain out, look it in the face, deal with it by feeling, and then her healing could begin.

She was hiding her feelings and her grades were suffering. She was unable to concentrate. Nothing seemed either happy or sad to her; everything had a blah feel. She had lost her affect. Interestingly, she was, though, using up a lot of energy to keep her emotions in check, so often she would tire easily, but not really know why. She didn't choose to talk with anyone about her problems since she felt she would just be burdening them. Therefore, she chose to keep them inside. She decided to really put her feelings under the rug, to bury them, and then just to move on in hopes that everything would be as it was before. However, that was impossible.

Once Becky's self-imposed iceberg started to melt a little, she became more vulnerable. And with that vulnerability, I was better able to reach her. She started to vent; I listened. She decided to write a poem about her feelings and shared that with me. By putting her feelings down on paper, she was able to really look at them, embrace them, and own them.

The healing did not happen automatically. Becky often felt as if she were on a roller coaster ride. But, finally, the ride began to get smoother and she started feeling better. Yes, Becky learned that feeling is healing.

***

What Grieving Feels Like

Each person grieves in his own way. For instance, when a family member dies, two teenagers are left to grieve. One chooses to cry a lot; the other chooses to go his own way. An outward display of emotion does not signify that you care any more than the person who does not openly express his grief.

Grieving is a continuous process. At first, you only feel the tip of the iceberg. You feel shock. Your body actually sends out chemicals and numbs your emotions. Eventually, the rest of the iceberg, the grief, comes above the surface and you will start to feel more and more. Then, as you start to deal with your grief, the iceberg will start to melt and you will be left with a bunch of emotions that will stay for a while. Hang in there; you will deal with those and be able to go on with your life.

Some emotions you might feel

1. Numbness, then confusion …how will you survive? Added responsibilities may engulf you.

2. Sadness may permeate everything you do; your energy level will feel low.

3. Isolation may be felt; loneliness sets in.

4. Anger and unfairness fill you.

5. You may be filled with guilt and regret

The important thing is to remember to allow yourself to feel. Remember, you grieve with your heart, not with your head. You may try to think things through logically, but that just won't work. Your head understands that the person has died; your heart will not accept it, so you are filled with confusion. Be gentle with yourself.

The stages you will experience

1. You may just feel blah. Everything looks gray.

2. Numbness leaves, reality sets in and you just need to survive. During this stage, it is healthy to vent. Share your thoughts and feelings. Perhaps write a poem or a story concerning the one who has died. Perhaps make a collage of pictures. Memories help to heal.

3. Healing starts and you begin to feel better. This is a slow process and has its ups and downs.

4. You survive and realize that you will continue to survive.

Everyone needs to go through these stages to come out whole. Each person does have his own way to heal, but he must take time to allow this to happen. It is a painful process, but one that must be felt. Sometimes a person finishes with one stage only to return to it later, but in time, the person will be able to finally reach the last stage…acceptance…and move on with his life.

***

On the Outside Looking In

Susie was seated across from me. Looking imploringly at me she said, "But I don't belong. I feel so alone. They are my family, but they're not my family. Oh, Mrs. Cohen, what can I do?"

I thought about Susie, thought about her circumstances. She was living with her cousins; unfortunately she did not have parents with whom she could reside. Her cousins were nice, but she always felt as if she were on the outside looking in, even with her cousins' children.

Looking at Susie and then at my desk, I noticed my coffee cup and some paper clips. "Watch me, Susie, and I'll try to explain what I think is happening."

I took the cup and placing a paper clip in it I said, "Susie, this cup is the family unit and the clip stands for the people in the family. They are in their comfort zone...the family...the cup. Now watch. I will take another clip...this one is you...and I am going to place it outside of the cup. See?"

Susie looked and nodded. I proceeded to tell her that her cousins were all together in one unit. She felt excluded...she was still a clip...still a member of the family, but she was not part of the unit, she was not part of the comfort zone, the cup. Susie continued to look at my example and then at me. I could see she was starting to understand the analogy. Actually, often I find it is helpful to use objects to explain things so the youngster can visually see what I mean.

From my display, a conversation ensued. It seems that Susie does not feel that she is like her cousins. She feels they are smarter, more athletic, more popular, etc. and because of this she does not feel she has much in common with them. She doesn't call their parents, Mom and Dad. They are not her mom and dad so she doesn't want to call them that and in her mind that makes a distinction right there. So yes, there is a wall and that wall does keep her out of the cup.

I suggested that perhaps her cousins all sense Susie's feeling of alienation, her sense of not being sure of her place in the family. Therefore, they do not want to smother her and make her feel even more uncomfortable than she already feels. Yet, by giving her a lot of space, they are unwittingly making her feel like an outsider.

"You know, Susie, I really think you need to tell them how you feel. You need to reach out to them; then they will hopefully reach out to you. Right now they probably are feeling a little alienated, too, and really don't know what to do. However, they probably are afraid of hurting your feelings so they are saying nothing. But just think...it's kind of like a traffic jam...everything has come to a stop and no one is moving forward. Someone has to start his car and then the rest will be able to follow. Do you understand what I mean? Does this make sense to you?"

We then continued to talk about her biological parents. Unfortunately they were not in the picture; however, they never would be, so Susie had to accept this and move on.

Continuing our talk, I said, "Just because you don't call your cousins, Mom and Dad, does not mean that they cannot treat you as Mom and Dad. A title does not make the person. A person's actions and thoughts, his caring ways, those are what define him as a parent. Names, honey, are not important; it's the deeds that count."

Next, we talked about her interests and how they differed from her cousins; yet, through our discussion we also realized they had some interests in common. They loved music, they loved mall shopping, and they liked reading.

"Try having conversations with your cousins. Use your common interests as starting points. Then, talk about their interests, too. Susie, you don't have to be good in sports, but you can still go to their games and cheer. Then, you will be able to discuss the games with them. They can go to some of your musical concerts. In other words, open yourself up to them and they, in turn, will open themselves up to you. What do you have to lose? Give it a try."

I am hopeful that it will work for Susie, that she will be able to be on the inside of the unit with the rest of her cousins, rather than on the outside looking in. She will be able to reestablish herself as a viable member of the family and in so doing, she will be able to shed her despair and become a more content person, a person who will be filled with a sense of warmth and security, only obtainable through being on the inside.

***

The Girl on the Island

Looking out my office door, I noticed Sheila sitting on a chair with her head in her hands. Realizing that I was her counselor, I quickly exited my office, approached her and ushered her in my door. I told her to have a seat and to take a few breaths.

Then, I softly asked her, "What's the problem?"

Looking up through her tear stained eyes, Sheila simply said, "I guess I am having a bad day."

I told her that if she could voice the problem, we could then look at it, decide what to do about it, and start managing it. Finally, Sheila began to tell her story.

A ninth grader, Sheila came to the high school with the anticipation of having a wonderful time. Unfortunately, she has found after just a few weeks of school that that has not been the case. Her so-called best friend does not like her anymore; her boyfriend now has eyes for someone else; her schoolwork has been suffering. To add to this litany of woe, her sister is making her life miserable by always picking on her and borrowing her clothes without permission to do so. Sheila is feeling alone, with no one to whom she can vent her problems.

We decided to write down these troubling situations and to deal with them one at a time. Otherwise, they seemed to be too daunting when taken as a total package.

We tackled friendship first. It turns out that her "best" friend stopped talking to her over something very trivial. After examining the issue, we realized that Ashley was not really a friend if she chose to dump Sheila the way she had.

"Sheila," I said, "you are just a freshman; there are about 300 students in your class. Try to meet some other friends in your class, invite them home, and start hanging with them. Do you belong to any clubs or athletic teams? You can always make new acquaintances that way."

Sheila told me that she does not participate in any extra-curricular activities. "How can I make friends, Mrs. Cohen? I mean I really don't see anyone after school and there are only a few minutes for passing between classes. And at lunch, I don't want to sit anywhere near Ashley and I don't really know the other girls that are not sitting with her."

"Ah, Sheila. You know you're like a gal on an island. Everyone else is together on the mainland and you are stuck on the island all alone, feeling a little sorry for yourself. I suggest you start to swim over to the mainland. You need to reach out to others and they will reach out to you. You need to not be alone. Loneliness brings on despair and gives you time to have you own little pity party."

We talked about this for a while and Sheila did agree that she had to start widening her circle. She told me that she was working in a group in English class and perhaps would invite one of the members of her group to come to her house. Readily I agreed with her plan of action.

"You know, Sheila, once you start making some new friends, even your older sister won't seem to be such a pain. Right now, you're unhappy, so everything is getting to you. You're so consumed with your loneliness that you're using all your energies thinking about that situation and you're not putting any energy into finding new friends. You really have to try to join some groups, and make it happen. Everyone needs somebody and it's always good to have more than one friend. I think you feel a little depressed; everything is starting to get to you. The only way to get through this is to stop dwelling on the way you feel now and push yourself. It won't be easy, but if you have a conscious desire to change, you will change. So, leave that self-imposed island and start your swim to shore where you will find other people with whom you can be friendly."

***

The Girl in the Igloo

Actually, I did not go to Alaska and I did not actually see a girl in an igloo, but the image is appropriate. Holly was getting violent headaches, so violent that nothing seemed to quell the pain until she would retire for the night. Then, after a restless sleep, Holly would awaken with no pain, only to have it return gradually during the day. And so the cycle would continue. Her parents brought her for tests, yet nothing could be found to explain the headaches.

Once a very good student, Holly started to do poorly in school. She had difficulty concentrating and remembering material that she had learned. Once active in sports, Holly was now a spectator. Her head hurt too much. One doctor suggested that perhaps tension could be causing her headaches and he gave her the name of a therapist.

Holly went to the therapist, discussed some issues, and found that if anything, her headaches were exacerbated from the meetings. She stopped the sessions. Holly probably did that because she didn't want to experience more pain. The therapist was trying to get Holly to expose her issues, but Holly just wasn't ready to do that.

Actually, Holly really didn't seek me out; I had called her into my office after warnings had been issued. This very bright gal was not performing well and I was concerned. I knew about the headaches and knew she had gone to see different professionals.

Sitting across from me, Holly filled me in on the details and the results of the tests. As she spoke, I could see the anxious look on her face. Looking at her lap, I noticed she was twisting her hands. Gently, I queried her about her friends and family. She smiled when she spoke about some of her close friends and even told me that she seemed to sleep more soundly at their homes. Well, that gave me food for thought. So I asked her why she thought she slept better there than at home.

She looked behind her to make sure my door was closed, then answered slowly, thinking through what she had to impart. "You know, Mrs. Cohen, my folks are either yelling at each other or yelling at me and you know what, I really have no idea sometimes what they are even yelling about."

"What do you do when that happens?" I asked.

"To tell you the truth," she continued, "I used to answer their yelling, I used to question why they were angry and sometimes I would even start yelling, but then I thought, why bother, my questions don't get any appropriate responses. Instead, I feel like a really bad person and the yelling intensifies. So, now I just walk away and go to my bedroom and shut the door. I just don't want to hear the yelling."

We discussed her method of dealing with the upsetting moments at home and I helped her to see that instead of dealing with the issues, she was running away from them all because she didn't know any other way to deal with them. Leaving the scene had become her modus operandi. Yet, she really hadn't dealt with the yelling, so the intense feelings that the yelling had caused were now bottled up inside of her. She was not able to let them out, yet her body wanted to do so.

"You know, Holly, our body is sort of like a balloon that is being filled with air. If some of that air does not seep out, what happens?"

"It will pop!"

"Right!" I responded, "And that's what's happening to you now. I mean you're not actually popping, but your head is hurting badly. That's your body's way of reacting. I truly believe that the body and the mind are related. So, unless you want to go on having headaches, you must come to grips with your feelings and learn to deal with your existing home issues. It seems to me that your parents are not going to change, so you are the one who is going to have to change your coping skills."

Holly thought for a few minutes. Clearly she was agitated and couldn't see any clear solutions, so I suggested a few. She could write her parents a letter detailing how she feels. She could go out with them to a restaurant and talk to them. They probably would not yell there. She could ask them if she could stay with a friend for a while or with an older sibling who no longer lived at home. She could vent her feelings to her friends. She could keep a diary or she could write down her feelings and then rip up the paper or even burn it.

"Whatever you think will work, Holly, try. I do know that you must vent your feelings somehow, otherwise your body will continue to hurt as it searches for some relief."

Holly had never chosen to share her feelings about anything, since when she had done that at home, she had gotten into trouble, so, in fact, she now was like a girl in an igloo. She had surrounded herself with impenetrable ice so that no one could reach her and upset her. She had closed off her feelings to others. However, now her body was negatively responding. Her headaches were debilitating. It was apparent that the igloo she had constructed was going to have to melt. Holly was going to have to let people in.

The bell rang, the period was ending and Holly had to get to class.

As she left, I looked her in the eye, smiled and said, "Holly, thanks for sharing. Now there is a small crack in that igloo. Let's see if you can't make the crack even larger. Your headaches should lessen, and you should be able to put your efforts into your schoolwork, rather than into just being able to exist. Get back to me and let me know how you are doing."

***

Drugs, Alcohol, Eating Disorders, Pregnancy

To Complete the Puzzle, All the Pieces are Needed

Tom came into my office, looking very forlorn. Grades were down, his appetite was down and his head was down. We talked for a while, not much surfaced, but I did tell him that I was going to have his mom come in and together the three of us would sit down and try to understand what was occurring.

Tom's mom arrived the next day. A lovely and articulate woman, she shook my hand and then took a seat directly across from my desk. We exchanged pleasantries and then I called in Tom. Interestingly enough, he entered, grabbed a seat and then moved it as far away as possible from Mom. Naturally, I noticed, since I often find gestures more telling than words.

Looking at his permanent record card, it was obvious that something in his life must have occurred during 8th and 10th grade. Those are the years that showed a decline in grades. Mom was convinced that grades plummeted because of poor study habits and a dislike of school, yet if this were so, why would Tom have succeeded during the other years?

I looked to Tom and his mom for an answer, but no one seemed to have one. I talked about Tom's home life. Something had to be going on or I didn't think he would have pushed the chair away. I also harped on his 8th grade and 10th grade marks and told both to really search their memories for what had transpired.

When nothing was forthcoming, I set up a study plan for Tom, put him on progress reports, gave Tom a pass to his class, and said goodbye to Mom, thanking her for coming in. Yet, clearly I wasn't happy. Something had to have happened during those two years, something that was still nagging at Tom and stopping him from really doing well in school. But what and how could I find it out?

Being a persistent person, I waited a day and then I called Tom into my office. He sat across from me, with an expectant look in his eyes, and seemed to be silently saying, "Now what?"

We started talking and I asked him if he liked puzzles. Looking at me quizzically he responded, "Sometimes, but I do get annoyed if I can't complete them."

"You know, Tom, I feel the same way. I get upset when I can't put all the pieces together and right now, that's how I feel with your problem. I have this puzzle to do, yet I can't and it's not because I am not trying. It's because I don't have all the pieces. Let me discuss the pieces I do have and then maybe you can present me with the others."

I got to tell you, it wasn't easy. Tom tried to look everywhere, but at me, yet I smiled sympathetically, and gently pushed him for a response. Finally, Tom took a deep breath and started sharing with me. It seems his dad is an alcoholic, something never ever mentioned by the family. Mom and his other brothers try to pretend the problem doesn't exist, yet it does and Tom's life has been on a roller coaster ride. He shared with me problems that surfaced in 8th and 10th grade and problems that are still occurring today. During Tom's 9th grade, Dad was going to AA and doing much better. So, the house was a happier place and so was Tom.

Now, with the economy doing poorly, Dad has been laid off from his job and has been turning to liquor as his salvation. Only it is not his salvation; nor is it the salvation for the others in the family. It's hell! Some days Dad is fine; other days he's in a lousy mood. He picks on everyone, so everyone just tries to stay out of his way. The tension in the house is unbearable at times.

"But, Mrs. Cohen, what can I do? I mean no one wants me to talk about this. Mom couldn't talk to you in your office, and everyone would be very upset with me if they knew that I voiced the family secret. Some days, I just don't even feel like going home, yet he is my dad and I love him. I feel guilty that I feel this way. He can be such a good father. Do you understand what I am saying?"

Looking at him, I softly replied, "Yes, I do, and you know what, I am so proud of you for sharing things with me. I know you love your dad, but I also know you hate his actions. Now, I have the pieces I need to finish the puzzle and once it's completed, we can take a good look at all the pieces and try to get together a plan of action."

Tom and I are still trying to work things out. I talked to him about Alanon, and Alateen, support groups that he could choose to attend. I told him that we have groups at school, too. On the home front, he and his brothers are going to try to have an intervention with Dad. They realize that the secrecy, the denial, has to stop. They realize that until all the pieces of the puzzle are out there for everyone to look at, the family will never be healthy and whole. Perhaps things will work out. Tom has made the first step by admitting that the problem exists.

***

There Are Certain Things You Cannot Change

It was sunny outside, but inside my office it was definitely dark and gloomy. Jessica was seated across from me. After dissolving into tears, she had been ushered into my office by her classroom teacher. I told her to take a few breaths, calm down and tell me what was troubling her. Wringing her hands, then reaching for a tissue, Jessica squirmed in the chair, took some breaths, tried to gain composure and then looked up at me to speak.

"Mrs. Cohen," she said haltingly, "My mom is an alcoholic."

With that she started to cry again, so I patiently waited for her to continue.

"I just don't know what to do. Sometimes she is fine; at other times, she comes in the house so drunk that she is incapable of helping me to do anything and when I do attempt to do something, she finds fault with me and yells."

I asked her if she had talked to her dad about this.

"Yes, but he can't do anything. He has threatened to leave her; I think he just stays around because of us. Do you know she makes promises and breaks them? She tells me to meet her at a certain time and then she doesn't show up. I can't trust her. The funny thing is I do love her, but I am so embarrassed. I try not to bring my friends home since I never know what I am going to find. I don't want her to meet me at a game because I don't know what condition she will be in. What can I do? Please help me!"

Now that Jessica had put her cards on the table, we were able to look at them to see what we could do.

"You know, Jessica, you do not have the power to change your mom. So what you have to do is decide what you can do about you. Instead of your mom's situation controlling you, it is time for you to control how you will react and what you will choose to do. Obviously Mom is not ready to change, but you can do some things to give you coping skills."

Then I proceeded to tell Jessica about Alateen, a program for teenagers whose parents have a problem with drugs and alcohol. Also, I told her that we hold a meeting at school that she may wish to join.

"Not that it makes it any easier for you, Jessica, but there are other kids here who share your problems and concerns. At least you can share issues with them, learn what works for them, and start a healing process."

I gave her the names of our home-school adjustment counselors and our school psychologist and told her that our doors are always open to help her.

"Mrs. Cohen, it is so hard. Look what Mom has done to our family. Why can't she just be the mom I want her to be?"

"Well, Jessica," I answered, seeing the pain in her face, "while Mom is under the influence of alcohol, it is the alcohol that is determining her actions; it is not Mom. Do I wish she could change? Absolutely! But she won't do that until she is ready. She has to hit bottom first and obviously she has not done that. Just hold onto the thought that addiction is hard to beat. Mom has an illness; do try to understand that. That does not mean that you have to accept what she is doing, but try to forgive her. It will make it easier for you in the long run. I know this is not an easy situation for you, but you can learn from it and realize that you just don't have the power to change Mom. What you do have the power to change is you."

***

Okay, so your kid is using...now what?

You suspect that your kid is using. What to do? First of all, confront him with the evidence without yelling and screaming. He will probably deny that he is using anything and even though you may have found some stuff in his room, he will probably tell you that he doesn't know how it got there. Duh????

Hang in there and keep hounding. Tell him that you are taking him to the doctor's for testing. Pot will stay in his system for 30 days; some of the other stuff is hard to really trace. But just telling him that you will be taking him to a doctor's shows him that you mean business!

You can look in the phone book, in the yellow pages, and find counseling services and hot lines usually listed under Alcoholism Treatment or Drug Abuse Treatment. Don't be afraid that maybe you are making too much out of the whole deal. It is better to overreact than not to react at all. Before you see the counselor, do write down all the pertinent information...family history, drug-abuse history, your suspicions, and any prior treatment plans.

It will probably have to be you who insist that your child seek treatment. Perhaps you can ground your kid until treatment is sought. Perhaps you can take away the car, phone and/or TV privileges…whatever works to get him to seek help. Remember, this is not the time to be soft. Assistance is needed and you are the one who must be tough, who must make certain that your child's needs are met. Don't let him con you and tell you that he will never use again.

Trust me, that won't happen. He will use again and again until he admits he has a problem, addresses it and seeks help. And you are not the professional. You are the intermediary, the one who will take him to the professional. Sometimes with all your insistence, your child will not seek and get the appropriate help, but at least you will have tried.

Unfortunately, with many kids, help is not sought until they have really reached bottom and are desperately hurting. Counselors all seem to agree on one point. What works as far as treatment is concerned is the involvement of the parents. They have to be part of the process. Usually using drugs is the child's way of crying out to others that he needs help. So make sure you accompany your child to the therapist. If he needs in house treatment, make certain that you go to the parent meetings. Show your child that you are there for him, that you care, and that together you will strive to fight the drug demon that is ruining and running his life.

Make sure you tell him that you love him. You know that drug abuse and addiction are life threatening. There is hope; he can get better. It is so important that you share this hope with him since many times kids are afraid to get help. They don't want to give up using, since they feel that they will not be able to cope with life without the crutch of drugs. They are scared and they should be. They are taking a big step forward. They are giving up a comfort zone, albeit a destructive one. What will they find?

Once treatment has begun, this will be a very difficult time for you and your family. Your child may become very irritable. He may outwardly say that he hates you. But inwardly I truly believe he will be relieved to know that you do care. Hang in there. Better times will be coming and when they do, the nightmare will be over and you will once again be a family that functions in a healthy and productive way. It will not be a quick process; it will take time. And one counselor may not work; you may have to seek another one. But don't give up. Keep plodding ahead.

Don't be afraid to reach out for help yourself. There is an organization called Tough Love that many parents have found beneficial. You may want to give them a call.

A lot of blaming will go on. "What did I do to cause him to use drugs?" A lot of "if onlies" will go through your mind. Just remember, blame should not be placed on anyone. Blame stops people from reacting. It sort of keeps you right there under a cloud. Instead, there is no blame. The problem just exists. Now is your time to do positive things, to get help, not to do negative things and blame.

There is light at the end of the tunnel, but you have to travel through the darkness in order to reach it. Good luck.

***

Rescue Fantasy

I have been thinking a lot about that phrase lately, especially since I am now in the last throes of dealing with my seniors and hoping that they will graduate, choose the right paths on which to continue their lives, and eventually be all that they can be. Big order, I know. Anyway, in so wishing and wanting so desperately for all of this to take place, I think I have gotten into some of their faces a little too much.

Intellectually, I tell myself that I have given them the tools, now they have to take those tools to build their futures. However, emotionally, I sometimes seem to do otherwise and keep leading them and pushing them in the hopes that they will succeed. Ah…but here's the rub…am I pushing them to succeed the way I want them to succeed or am I listening to what they want and then pushing them to reach their chosen goal? Am I giving them space to really search for the best way to reach that goal? Unfortunately, sometimes I am probably clinging to my fervent wishes. Don't we all do that to some degree?

Let's take a look at a common scenario. Your son has been in trouble with drinking and drugging. He feels he is using drugs recreationally and it's okay to do so. After all, he wants his friends to think he's cool; they use and seem to do okay, so why can't he? You try to reason with him. You tell him using drugs is illegal. They are adversely affecting him. He seems to be more moody and his grades are poor. You try to tell him that if his friends are really his friends, they will respect his wishes not to use. Yet, all your ranting and raving is to no avail. Rob keeps using and finally gets caught at school. You feel awful. Rob gets punished.

Time passes. He returns to school and continues to use. You ground him; you take away his car, TV and phone privileges. Use of the computer is curtailed. He tells you where you can go and seems to get more sullen. You reason that you are in his face for his own good. And this is true, but are you caught up in the "rescue fantasy"?

Do you feel that if you just get in his face one more time that he will stop using and become the old Rob that you once knew and desperately want to have around the house again? Yet, try as you might, you cannot rescue him; he seems even more determined to cling to his ways.

Finally, you come to the realization that you have to stop this rescue attempt; Rob has to accept responsibility for his actions and rescue himself. Until that happens, all that you do will not cause him to change and in fact, he may act out more just to get your goat. Painful as it may be, you will have to take a seat outside of the rescue realm and perhaps see him reach bottom – for as long as you keep rescuing him, he will never reach bottom and will never hurt enough to change.

What to do? Realistically, I think you should and do have the right to point out what you want and why you want it. Try to have a discussion, but I gotta tell you, if he is not willing to listen, then there is nothing more you can do except "bug off" and hope that he will seek out your assistance at a later date when he realizes that his only option on his road to positive accomplishments is to change.

So, if like me, you are sometimes caught in a "rescue fantasy", ask yourself if, indeed, it is a fantasy. If it is, use all your willpower to lay low until the rescue can become a reality.

***

How My Dictionary Has Changed!!!

When I was a kid in school, it was so different. Words had such different meanings from those today. Pot was something my mom would use for cooking. Coke was a drink I would have with my friends. A joint was a little place to hang out in sometimes. A weed was something I would pull out of the garden. Gay meant that I was happy. Stoned meant some kind of work that was done on the front of a house. High usually meant something that was way up there. Get my drift? Times have changed, and with the changing times, kids have changed. There is not only new lingo, but also the effect of the new lingo and new coping skills that are needed. As a parent what can you do?

Be aware. Be alert. Never feel that it cannot be your kid. Avoid denial. But how do you know if there is a problem? What should you look for? Hopefully, the following will help you.

1. A change of friends. Many times a teen who is troubled will be drawn to a group that is taking dangerous risks and is heavily committed to using alcohol and drugs.

2. Deterioration in appearance. Your child may be wearing grungy clothes. He may not care what he puts on.

3. An "I don't care" attitude. His affect is diminished. Nothing seems to excite him.

4. Poor performance in school, at home, and on the playing field drops. He does not seem to be able to follow through with anything.

5. Irritability and sensitivity are exacerbated. The user may become hostile, avoid family contact, overreact to mild criticism and tune out and leave when pressed for accountability.

6. Wide mood swings. He may seem happy one minute and very unhappy the next minute.

7. Disappearance of money, pills, alcohol and other personal belongings. You notice they are gone, but do not wish to think he has taken them.

8. Lying. If you confront him, he will make excuses about most situations that have occurred.

9. Trouble with the law. He may be caught using, having drugs on his person, selling, speeding in his car, or doing other unlawful things.

What are the visual clues?

With alcohol

1. Physical –red eyes, headaches, unsteadiness, sleepiness, alcohol on the breath

2. Behavioral – sleeping too much, fighting, arguing, uninhibited behavior

With marijuana (pot)

1. Physical – red eyes, fatigue, apathy, hunger, cough, chest pains, silly grin

2. Behavioral – no motivation, poor grooming, mood swings, arguments, poor grades, attention problems, more mellow than usual

With cocaine

1. Physical – dilated pupils, runny nose, hoarse voice, increased sensitivity to light, sweating, pale complexion

2. Behavioral – rapid mood changes, unexplained anger, sleeping patterns confused, memory problems, depression

Parents sometimes say, "Hey, he doesn't really have a problem. All kids experiment." This may be true, but use may lead to abuse that may lead to addiction. Take a look at the steps to addiction.

1. Exploration –he will just give drugs a try

2. Enjoying the mood swing – he likes the mood drugs cause and wants it again

3. Seeking the mood swing more often- he needs the drugs more and more

4. Keeps thinking about getting high and drunk; gets obsessed…life revolves around how to get the stuff, where to use it, and how to use it; nothing else matters

5. Finally he must need the drugs to feel normal. This now is called chemical dependency. This is addiction. The drugs own him.

Yes, the vocabulary of today has changed and with it, our kids have changed. These times can be tough, so be alert and take appropriate action when that is needed.

***

When You Lie Down With A Dog Who Has Fleas

Ah, that title kind of gives you pause, doesn't it? And you know how the sentence ends? Yup, you come up scratching!

I just finished giving that piece of information to a young man who was in my office. I had received so many discipline sheets on him. He has been cutting classes, acting out in some of them, and not earning good grades.

"What's the deal?" I asked him, getting right to the point as I always do.

And like most other kids, he hemmed and he hawed and seemed to have really no idea as he shrugged his shoulders and gave me a half smile. We began to talk about the kids he hangs with...the ones he calls his friends. And, not surprisingly, they, too, have been skipping school and getting into other kinds of trouble. Interesting eh? As with so many things, water does seek its own level. Perhaps that's why this bunch of kids is attracted to each other. But does it have to be that way?

Joe and I talked for a while. I explained to him that when you pal with someone who is acting out, it gives you license to act out. The following is the gist of what I said to him...

You figure, if your friend can act that way, well then, so can you. Besides, you don't want him to consider you a dork, so you go along with the crazy pranks, you choose to look the other way when things are not done correctly, and as far as schoolwork is concerned, you choose not to do it. I mean, he doesn't, so why should you? Besides, you don't want him to think you're a nerd if you get good grades.

Whoa, stop right now. Reassess your thoughts. Number one, do consider the word pal and the word friend. What kind of a pal or friend is this who gets into trouble and eggs you on? Yeah, it might seem like fun for the moment, but what are the consequences? Shouldn't a good friend be a positive role model for you, be someone who cares about your welfare, and impresses upon you that it is right to do the correct thing? Shouldn't a good friend be someone with whom you feel proud to have as a friend, someone who is highly thought of, who wears a good name?

What you are not thinking about is how contagious friends are; when they misbehave, you misbehave. When they goof off, you goof off. When they think school is not cool, you begin to think it's not cool. When they start to do drugs and

109

tell you how good they will make you feel, then you start to do them, too. After all, if they work for your friend, they will work for you, too. Besides, these are your friends. You want to be with them. You want to be part of the group and feel the comfort of belonging.

What to do? For starters, reassess your choices. I know that's hard to do, but you have to do it You need to be good to yourself and that means you have to hang with people who will be good for you. Remember, I said friends are contagious, so you want to pal with good ones so good stuff will rub off on you. I think after a while you will find that it is okay to get good grades, it is cool to stay in school, and it is right to be clean from drugs. It won't be easy to change friends; they were your comfort zone, but actually they were providing a misery zone.

So, Joe, do some soul searching. Do you want to lie down with a dog who is wagging his tail, who obeys, who is clean and healthy, or do you want to lie down with one who growls and has fleas? Think about it and then act accordingly.

***

A Young Woman's Journey Back From Drugs

Jean Bean, not her real name, came into my office the other day. I was so thrilled to see her. The whites of her eyes glistened like new fallen snow. Her face was radiant and blushed with good health. Her figure was trim and her posture was straight as an oak tree. She wished to change her schedule for next term in order to take a more challenging course. Her grades were good and she felt she would be able to tackle an additional course.

Sounds like a typical occurrence? Wrong! You see, just 2 ½ years ago, when I first met Jean Bean, she was very heavy, was failing all her courses, had brown eyes that were surrounded by a sea of pink, and wore a sullen expression. Her clothes did nothing to camouflage her heaviness and she definitely looked unkempt. So, why the change?

Well, I asked her just that question.

"Mrs. Cohen, I guess it's because I finally decided to stop using drugs."

"Just like that?" I countered. "Come, stay for a while and tell me the road you've been traveling. Then, maybe I can write about it, others can read it and maybe your experience will touch a few lives and change them. What do your say?"

Readily agreeing, Jean took a seat across from me. I picked up a pencil and took a piece of paper, and began to record her journey from addiction to recovery, from darkness to light, from despair to hope and from weakness to strength.

It all began when she was about ten years old. Her brother, older than she, introduced her to pot. She would toke up outside the house, hang with his friends and listen to their merriment. By the time she was thirteen she was doing pot regularly. Often, she would get it for nothing from one of her girlfriend's brothers. Soon, Jean was getting acid and mushrooms and using them. She would get high, get in trouble at school, skip classes, get suspended, and continue using.

Then, her brother was in an accident and died, her father moved and Jean went into a deep depression. To Jean, drugs were her only salvation. Yet, actually, they were her destruction and she found herself in trouble with the police.

Domestic violence occurred, she was removed from her home and placed in a rehab facility. This happened twice and at the end of her second confinement, Jean was released to her sister. Finally, it was decided that she should move to Massachusetts and live with her father.

Welcome to high school and to Mrs. Cohen! Sizing up the situation, Jean immediately made friends with those people who could keep her habit alive. Still depressed from her brother's death and still heavy and filled with stress, Jean Bean felt she needed drugs to survive. Her grades plummeted. Summer came and her problems and habit continued.

Back in school for 10th grade, Jean was now in classes where she started to improve and feel a little better. However, in the middle of the year, she became involved with drugs and she left school. From February on, she worked. During the summer, she took a good look in the mirror and did not like the image she saw. She would take drugs, feel good, but then go into a depression as the drugs left her system. Then, the cycle would repeat itself. Jean told herself that she could not continue in this manner, but how could she change?

Her father and she moved to a new neighborhood that allowed her to make new friends. Curtailing her use of drugs, she found that the pounds started melting away and soon she had lost 85 pounds. She found that with her physical self improving, her mental self was improving. She was able to grapple with her brother's death and although she still missed him, she was able to get on with her life. Her depression had lifted. The drugs were no longer needed. Thinking clearly, Jean now knew that she must return to school and get herself on the right path.

At the end of the summer, she approached the Principal and told him that she wished to "return to school in order to be able to get a better future."

She told me, "The Principal was great; he really listened to my side of the story and my willingness to change and decided to let me return to school. Now I knew I had the chance I wanted and that it was up to me not to mess up that chance. I had to make the most out of this opportunity."

Well, unfortunately, Jean met up with some kids while she was in school who enticed her to use heroin.

"They told me that it made them feel so good. They actually persuaded me to use it."

Well, Jean's bad self started to return. Her depression surfaced and she started to lose interest in others and herself. Her old symptoms had returned. She would feel paranoid from doing drugs. She would feel all "sketched" out. She would feel that someone was out to get her.

After two weeks, she awakened to reality and vowed to stop using. She decided to make goals, to stay clean, and to keep her commitment to herself and the Principal to finish high school. Jean began to do a lot of reading and soul searching. She began to take time for herself, to make herself look good so she would feel good. She decided to attend AA meetings and found strength and support. There, people understood her; they had taken a similar journey.

Looking at me with a smile on her face she said, "You know, Mrs. Cohen, I finally did a 180 and I've stayed that way. Now I have all passing grades, mostly B's. My self-esteem is better. I have confidence in myself. I choose to do what is right. When friends ask me to skip, I tell them no. I just don't want to. I need to get on with my life; I need to get on with my education. I have found strength and become free."

"Yes, I can see you are doing that," I gently responded, "But tell me, Jean, what kind of message do you have for other kids who may find themselves using and don't want to or don't know how to stop?"

She thought for a moment and then slowly responded, " I would tell them to be your own person. Don't be a follower. Believe in yourself. It is so much easier to be good than to be bad. It is hard to be bad. When you're bad, you always have to figure out a plan how you'll get away with things. Then one problem leads to another. If you get in trouble, do learn from it. Don't repeat past mistakes or dwell on them. They happened and you can't change them, but you can change where you are now. You know, Mrs. Cohen, my father went through two years of hell with me, yet he stood by me with disciplining, loving, caring and reasoning. He never gave up on me. I love him so much. He has helped me to survive. Now, I make good choices and he is supportive of me and proud of me. He always tells me that tomorrow is not always promised, so live today fully and have no regrets."

"Yes, Jean," I look at her and smile, "you are now living life fully and I am proud of you. Thanks so much for sharing your journey with me. My wish is that you continue to have no regrets."

***

Regrets

Yes, so many times kids come into my office sharing regrets with me. They talk about them, talk about them, and talk about them. It's like hearing the same record played over and over, and just like what is imprinted on the record, what is imprinted in history will not go away. What was done is done and cannot be erased. They can choose to keep talking about it, but will that help or will they just be digging it into the ground? And the deeper it is dug, the more firmly it becomes entrenched. It will finally take over every waking thought and interfere with daily living.

When kids have used drugs and have suffered the consequences, they naturally have regrets. They rehash what they have done, and why they have done it. They try to blame others for their prior use. Then they realize that they only have themselves to blame. They hurt; they are ashamed. They wish they could undo what they did. They come to the realization that they have not only hurt themselves, but also they have hurt so many other people…people who have reached out and tried to help them. How can they put it all behind them? They are sorry for what they have done. They have regrets.

I am not saying that regrets should not be discussed. The situation should be discussed, looked at, and then dealt with. It happened. You should deal with it and then get on with your life; otherwise, I know from experience, that regrets will hang in there and continue to haunt you. They will own you and keep you from moving forward, from enjoying your life.

I know that sounds good on paper, but then how does one get over regrets? What does one do? I think you have to look at what you did, own it, make amends to those you feel you have wronged and say that you did what you did and maybe it was what you had to do at the time. Maybe it was a wrong choice, but now the events following it just have to play themselves out. You have to forgive yourself. You are human and human beings make mistakes.

Then, you have to start looking at the positives that you have done and take comfort in those. Be thankful for what you do have; do not dwell on what you can't change. Will anything be accomplished by playing your regret over and over again in your mind? As you do hit instant replay, shut off the button and try listening to something else. Don't let one tune haunt you.

Push forward with every fiber of your being. I know it isn't easy. I, too, have had regrets. I, too, have repeated things until not only the listener, but also even I am tired of hearing them, yet I know I must move forward. There is a whole life out there to be embraced and I have the power to either embrace it or not.

You will learn that just as the sun rises and sets, a new day will continue dawning and it is up to you to get up and greet that day. Although the days will keep coming, you will never be able to thoroughly enjoy them and to really reap what each one has to offer until you finally put your regrets to bed and move on, since replaying your regrets never solved anything. Positive action and recognizing what you do have will enable you to go forward.

***

Eating Disorders

In 1983, Bulimia and Anorexia Nervosa made national headlines with the death of Karen Carpenter. That tragedy brought the eating disorders out into the open and many people sought help. Yet, many more do not acknowledge their problem that continues to exist and damage their health.

Many more females than males suffer from the disease that may end in death. Bulimics gorge, and then vomit and these actions may lead to heart irregularities. Often, bulimics take laxatives to further get rid of the food they have consumed. Unlike Bulimics, Anorexics barely ingest enough nourishment to survive.

Because of their lack of proper nutrition, both types of eating disorders lead to health problems. The enamel on teeth wears away, peach fuzz develops on the face as nature's way to keep the body warm, periods often stop, hair begins to fall out, and stomach problems are common. Once these people are into recovery, health issues may continue to plague them throughout their lives.

Just why do people become anorexic and/or bulimic? The common theory is that eating is the one thing that people feel they can control. The afflicted are usually from affluent families, tend to be white, are frenetic, and perfectionists. They are whirling around from one activity to the next, they have to be perfect, and the tension mounts and mounts. To them, their lives seem out of control and the only thing they can control is their eating.

Many of these people have poor self-esteems. After all, they can never reach the perfection to which they are striving so they must not be "good" people; they must not be worthy. They actually begin to really dislike themselves. They look at themselves and see ugly ducklings. Although they may be the perfect weight, they perceive themselves as heavy. Even when they do become emaciated, they still think of themselves as heavy. Therefore, they still choose to not eat too much. They will order dinner, and then proceed to pick at the food and push everything around on the plate so it appears to the onlooker that they are eating. If they are confronted, they become defensive and are not ready to acknowledge that they have a problem.

Therein, lies one of the main dangers, denial. How can you get through to people with the illness if they will not admit to having a problem? The sufferers must take ownership of the problem in order to seek help and change. Even when they do seek help and do start to gain some weight, they become scared. As much as they want to be normal, their compulsive self is still making them try to hold on to the eating disorder and their healthy self is trying to pull them away, so they are under a lot of tension. When they do start to get better, they have to remain wary so they will not relapse.

Good help is out there. As a parent, it is important to seek out that help, but first you, too, must recognize that your child has a problem. Sometimes, if your youngster will not admit to the problem, you may be able to get some of her friends over and you and her friends can sit down and confront her. Often, with so many people around showing their care and concern, the youngster will start to emerge from her cocoon. To emerge is scary, but to stay insulated takes a lot of work and can be devastating.

Please, if you do suspect a problem and if you would like some guidance, call your child's counselor who can direct you to the appropriate people who are knowledgeable in working with eating disorders. Your child can be helped to cope with her problems and regain her health.

***

But He Said He Loved Me

One afternoon after school I had an appointment. Looking behind the desk at the receptionist, a flash of recognition overcame me. Was it really Jill? I peered a little more closely.

Jill must have felt my eyes upon her, since she looked up, stared at me for just a moment and then her face broke out into a wonderful smile, "Mrs. Cohen…it is you, isn't it? How are you? Are you still at the same school?"

"Yes," I responded, "I guess I just love it too much to leave. Touching lives like yours and trying to make a difference keeps me going. How have you been and how's the little one?"

The little one, I soon found out, is now almost finished with elementary school! Where have the years gone? It seems like only yesterday when a teacher sought me out and voiced her concerns about Jill.

"You know, Judy, I am really concerned about Jill. She is still one of my top students, but her affect just isn't the same. Then, too, I notice her look has changed. I don't know, she just seems to have gotten rounder. Do you think she's all right? Do you think she could be pregnant? Can you call her in and at least talk to her and try to find out what's going on? Then, get back to me. Please don't tell her that I came to see you."

With that, the teacher turned on her heels and left, leaving me to my own devices. What should I do? Obviously, I didn't have an option. I had to call in Jill.

I issued a pass and waited for what seemed like an eternity. I had no clue what I was going to say or do.

Looking up from my desk, I noticed the outside door opening and there stood Jill. Watching her as she approached me, I noticed that she did seem to have gained weight. Other than that, though, she looked the same. She took a seat across from me. I smiled and decided to get right to the point. I've always found being direct gets more responses and hones right in on the problem.

So, I began… " Jill, how are you doing? Is everything O.K.? I've noticed you in the hallways and to me you look as if you've gained some weight."

She shifted uncomfortably in her seat, looked down at her fidgeting hands, and then gazed up at me. "Yes, I suppose I have, but I don't know why. And I do seem to be tired all the time."

I looked at her sweater and there seemed to be a slight bulge under it. After pausing for just a brief moment, I decided to plow right ahead "Jill, does your stomach hurt?"

She said that it did and to this day I don't know why, but she proceeded to pick up the bottom of her sweater just a bit and there was a bulge.

"Jill, now I really need to ask you a question because I care, so don't take offense. Are you pregnant?"

She looked at me with disbelief written all over her face and quickly retorted, "Mrs. Cohen, just what kind of girl do you think I am? After all, I'm a senior, I'm almost done with school, my marks are great, and I'm looking forward to college."

"I know, Jill, but I'm concerned. Your stomach does look large. Are you having any medical problems?"

And so the conversation went. Finally, it became apparent that Jill had no clue that she could be pregnant.

She had been staining, didn't think anything about it, and because of that she did not think her period was late. She did notice that she had gained weight, but when you're in denial, you choose to not let yourself question certain things. I asked her some pertinent questions and found out that she had a boyfriend and that they had been intimate. Yes, she knew she probably should have abstained, but he told her not to worry and told her that he loved her. And so how could she be pregnant? Ah, youth…so trusting, so innocent.

Well, I gave her some phone numbers of agencies that she could go to in order to find out if she were pregnant and of course she could administer some home tests. But I really wanted her to connect with someone. I told her it was important that she make the appointment immediately.

Well, in a few days she did go to the clinic and you guessed it, the results were positive. The more unsettling fact was that she was five months pregnant and the baby was due around graduation.

Jill didn't want to tell her folks the news, but after talking and more talking she realized that she needed their support. Her folks were stunned but to their credit rallied around their daughter, Jill. Unfortunately, the boyfriend, the one who said he loved her, did not rally; instead he took a long walk in the opposite direction and never looked back!

Well, Jill continued to come to school each day and once a month she would see the doctor. As she continued to grow, her sweaters increased in size. Finally, graduation was almost upon us. Would Jill make it?

I remember the time clearly. The phone in my office rang. It was the beginning of June. Actually, it was 3 days before graduation. It was Jill's mom telling me that Jill was in labor. I told her to keep me informed and I would tell the administrators that Jill would not be part of the graduation ceremony. She had completed her work, she was eligible to graduate, but she would not walk across the aisle to get the diploma. Instead, Jill would be graduating into a new role, the role of parenthood.

As I stood across the desk from Jill and as the above memories faded from my brain, Jill and I continued our conversation. She had had the baby, a son, and she had spent the summer caring for him. The father never got into the mix.

"Mrs. Cohen, I so believed that he loved me. I was so naïve. I wish I could reach out to all the teenagers today and let them know all that I've learned. Parenthood is not easy; giving up one's youth is so hard. My folks were great and together we worked it out so I could attend a community college and earn a degree. But all I did was study, care for my son, go to school and sleep when I could. Dating was out of the question. Of course, I had to build up trust in men again anyway. But, (and with that she looked at me with her face beaming and held out her hand) I am now married to a wonderful guy and he has given my son and me his name. I do feel so fortunate."

Yes, I could see that Jill was now content, but what a road she has traveled! Luckily she had support from her parents, luckily she was able to juggle everything so she could further her education, luckily she has found a good man who has renewed her faith and trust, but what if...? At least this time, Jill knows that when her husband says, "I love you", he means it.

***

Divorce

The Stained Shirt

Terry came into my office. Her home life was in an uproar; a nasty divorce was going on. Terry was feeling a tremendous amount of pain. She just didn't understand how her parents could not love each other and wondered if they really still loved her. And if they really did love her, then why couldn't they stay together and work things out? She was clearly confused, upset and depressed. Her grades were slipping. She didn't want to socialize with her friends, attend classes or play sports. Instead, she was wallowing in self-pity and was not allowing anyone to help her.

She was seeing a counselor, but not really sharing too much information. The counselor tried to tell her that things at home were not her doing; Terry had not caused them, nor could she change them. She listened, but didn't really internalize what the counselor said. She just wanted all the pain to go away and for things to return to normal.

"Terry", I told her, "things will not return to the way they were. Your parents have nothing against you. They just do not want to live with each other. Believe me, they still love you very much. What you have to do, Terry, is accept what is happening. You don't have to truly understand it or tell yourself not to be hurt by it, but you must accept it in order to move along with your life."

Terry listened, but I could tell, she still was not ready to accept her parents getting a divorce.

We talked about her counselor's visits. "You know, Terry, when you have a favorite shirt and it has stains on it, what do you do?"

"That's easy, Mrs. Cohen, I wash the shirt."

"Yeah," I replied, "but sometimes the stains won't come out unless they are pretreated first. And you know what, your problems are like stains. They must be looked at, pretreated, and then and only then, can you wash them away."

I proceeded to tell her that in order to get rid of her pain, she must look deeply within herself, admit the pain, share it with her counselor, and then listen and discuss ways to cope with the pain. In other words, together they would be treating the stains.

The stains are present now, but they don't have to be permanent stains. It's how one chooses to deal with those stains that will allow them to be treated and to eventually disappear. But she had to talk about how she was feeling and once she could mention her hurt, really voice it, then she would be able to look at it and manage it and eventually put it to rest.

I shared with Terry that the road ahead would not be an easy one. The stains had been there for a while, but I knew with the appropriate care, they could be dealt with. Wallowing in self-pity would make her unable to react. She would not have any energy left to do well in school, socialize with her friends, or participate in outside activities. She had to stop feeling sorry for herself and allow herself to deal with the issues that were causing her pain. Then, and only then, could she start to feel better.

***

What Does Family Really Mean?

I looked up family in the Webster's Dictionary and found several meanings. One meaning is the one we always think of: "a social group composed of parents and their children"; another is "a group of individuals living under one roof and one head".

Frankly, I choose to think of the second definition as the real definition. I guess it's because I have seen and heard so much that now I firmly believe that family is not determined by blood relations. Let's look at two stories.

Sara comes into my office. Looking dejected, she pulls a chair out and sits in it backwards, hanging over the front and peering up at me.

"I know, Mrs. Cohen, you called me in because my grades have been going downhill, but you know what, I really don't care. No one seems to care, so I don't care. I mean like why should I bother? All that happens is I get yelled at no matter what I do."

With some careful questioning, since I didn't want to appear too intrusive, I was able to ferret out the entire story. And it wasn't a pretty one.

It seems Mom and Dad had divorced when Sara was quite small and Sara lived with Mom for just a few years. Unfortunately, Mom had some difficulties in her life and due to bad judgment, chose to soften her pain through drugs and alcohol. Needless to say, Sara was taken from Mom's home and placed in Dad's.

Dad had been used to being on his own; now he had a child to take care of and he really wasn't ready for the job. Dad's vocation was demanding and tension-provoking. He would come home all riled up and take out his frustrations on Sara. When Sara would misbehave, mental and physical abuse would ensue. As Sara got older, the abuse continued.

Finally Sara felt she had had it and chose to run away and live with some friends. Eventually, she lived in a foster home for a while. Well, time passed and Sara finally returned home. However, the emotional abuse still continued. Poignantly Sara told me that no one has ever hugged her or said that they loved her.

How does Sara cope? I'll tell you...and it's a sad commentary...she chooses to go within herself and just shuts everyone out. She chooses not to feel; when she does, it's too painful. So, I ask, does Sara truly live with family?

Now, we'll look at case number two. Sean's story is similar to Sara's. He, too, is from a divorced home. Unlike Sara, his parents are not users of drugs or alcohol; however, they are abusers. Both have abused him emotionally. Both, perhaps because of their own emotional scars, can find no room in their hearts for Sean or perhaps they just don't know how to show love and caring. Whatever...all I know is they have made his life miserable.

Then, real family entered into his life. Not "blood" family, but caring, involved people who were unafraid to reach out, to give the requisite hugs and encouragement and to take Sean into their home and hearts. Sean was offered a place to stay and decided to take it. Recently I asked him why.

He said simply, "I finally had to take control of my life. I realized I had let others control it."

So, Sean moved out. It has been five years. He's a happy camper, has great grades, good SAT scores and is looking forward to college. His wonderful "family" has encouraged him to feel good about himself, to hold his head high, and to go forward with a smile on his face, knowing that he is worthy of a good life.

There are so many stories like the two I have shared. Some have happy endings; some are still being written; some will probably never improve. However, from these stories I have learned, regardless of what Webster says, the true meaning for the word family.

Family means people who care, people who share, people who listen, people who hug and people who give you the strength, the courage, and the encouragement to feel good about yourself as you grow in an environment filled with warmth. Family does not need to be comprised of people related by blood; family needs to be comprised of people related by the tie that binds…love.

***

Why Do I Act the Way I Do?

A while ago, a young lady came into my office. "Mrs. Cohen, why do I do the things I do? I just don't understand it. My mother is so nice to me, works hard to give me so many things, and I just end up doing crazy things, yelling at her, and getting into trouble."

Mary was visibly upset. I told her to take a deep breath, and then to tell me a little bit about her family. From conversation, I learned that both parents had remarried and that she lived with her mother and stepfather. She felt she enjoyed a nice relationship with them, but still, she seemed to fly off the handle so easily and "get in their faces" all the time.

Next, she talked about her dad and stepmother. Here, there seemed to be a problem. She never has gotten that close to her stepmother and feels that her stepmother finds fault with her all the time.

Talking further, she explained that she does visit both homes, but does not feel she has a real relationship with her stepmother.

"Do you tell Dad how you feel?" I asked.

"No, I mean I wouldn't want to hurt his feelings; he obviously loves my stepmother."

I went on to tell her that I felt she should be sharing with him how she felt. Dad loves her and wants her happiness. Therefore, I felt he would listen and respond and no doubt dispel some of her thoughts.

She continued by telling me that she particularly acts out after she has left her father's house and has returned to her mother's house.

"Yes, Mary, I'm sure you do. Think about this for a minute. Perhaps you have allowed yourself to get upset at your dad's house, have not vented your anger there for fear of upsetting him, and now you have brought home that anger and are redirecting it toward your mother. What do you think?"

She pondered this for a moment and then shook her head slowly, agreeing with my explanation.

I told her, too, that perhaps she acts out in other ways, getting into trouble and saying things without thinking because she is so upset and has to get those feelings out somehow.

"Well, Mrs. Cohen, what can I do about this?"

Looking at her and smiling, I answered, "Mary, now that you know what the problem is, you can fix it. What I think you have to do is share your feelings with Dad and your stepmother. I bet your stepmother feels your stiffness and does not allow herself to get that close to you either. Perhaps she is really not finding fault with you, but rather she is making suggestions, yet you perceive her suggestions as negatives. Move in a little, share a little, and she will start opening up to you, too. Once you both develop a little give and take, the air should clear, no one will be walking on eggs, and you should start feeling better. Then, when you leave Dad's house, you won't be carrying any negative feelings with you to Mom's house. Mary, it is hard to go from one house to another. There are different personalities, different rules, and other different things that you must adjust to once you enter; however, by communicating your feelings, you should start to be able to handle things better."

***

Children from Divorced Homes…Their 10 Commandments

So many kids come in to see me with problems and so many of these problems emanate from the fact that their parents are divorced or separated. If they could write this column, I think these would be the points that they would want you to remember.

1. You did not divorce me; you divorced my parent. So, please, even though I may not live with you, do invite me to join you sometimes. I still want to be in your life and communicate with you.

2. When we do go out, I do not always want to have your significant other join me; I need to have you just to myself so we can talk.

3. When you see me at a public function with your former spouse, do not yell and scream; your anger does not involve me, so I do not have to hear it. When you do, you embarrass me.

4. Don't try to buy my love by showering me with gifts that my other parent cannot afford.

5. Hugs, kisses, caring and sharing are the kinds of gifts I want. I may not always understand you, but I will always care about you.

6. Since you are not living at home, do give me a phone number where I can reach you. Sometimes I need to reach out and talk to you. Do pick up the phone and call me, too.

7. How I see you act is how I may choose to act; after all, your actions give me license to act in the same manner. I am still your child and need your guidance.

8. Please do not expect me to be with your family for all the holidays; I have to share my time.

9. Do not give me messages to deliver to your ex; do deliver them yourself.

10. Just because you are feeling pain does not mean that I am not feeling pain. I need to know that you still care about me. My family is split apart and I am unhappy but I do love you.

***

Who Will Take Care of the Caretaker?

I saw Karen in the hallway. There she was, deep in conversation with her arm around Ginny who was clearly upset. Karen was doing her usual thing – reaching out to someone, listening to her and helping smooth her ruffled feathers.

A few days passed. Again, I saw Karen. She was collecting information for someone. Again, she was in the helping mode and she was helping with a smile on her face and sprightliness in her step.

Later, Karen came into my office. We talked a little about her home life. I ascertained that she is the oldest of four. Mom is a divorced and single mom and Karen often takes care of her younger brothers and sisters. Because she is the oldest, she is often called upon to do household duties and work outside of the home. Not a complainer, Karen has accepted these roles. At times, when Mom has come home upset with work and life in general, it is Karen to whom she turns.

In school, Karen is very involved and does everything to perfection. Lauded by her peers and teachers, Karen seemingly has it all, or does she?

Karen is the hero of the family, the "do-gooder", the achiever, the person to whom family and friends turn when there's a favor to ask or a problem to share. Yet, let's really take a good look at our hero.

During the day, Karen develops headaches. From time to time, her stomach becomes upset. Looking at her hands, one can see that her cuticles are ragged. Does she pick at them? If Karen does not receive an A, she is in to see the teacher to see how to improve. She dwells on her "low" grade and really pushes to do better. When one looks at all of this, it is apparent that Karen is a caretaker who needs some "caretaking" herself.

It's hard to always be so perfect; it's hard to always be there for others; it's hard to always give and not receive. Yet, one may ask, why does she not complain? Well, verbally she's not complaining, but her body certainly is feeling the effects of Karen's being a caretaker.

Karen, like so many other heroes, is so intent on being so perfect that she never has time to take a breath and figure out if she is having fun yet. Being perfect has become her identity, so to keep herself intact as Karen, she must continue to excel.

Mom, being a divorced mom, is busy with her own issues. Karen knows that Mom works hard to keep the family together, so she does not want to bother Mom with her problems.

What will happen? One day, she may just get really depressed, tired and burned out. Physical ailments may become worse. Many heroes become anorexic; they can't control getting perfect grades all the time, but they can control what they eat. And always being in control is key to the "hero".

Hopefully, when she will hurt enough, she will recognize that hurt and seek help. Or, maybe a friend, sibling or parent will recognize her physical signs for what they are…manifestations of stress…and someone will reach out to be Karen's caretaker. Someone will give her license to make a mistake, to not be so hard on herself, to receive as well as to give. Someone will realize that he has to take care of the caretaker.

***

Divorce...Remarriage...Repercussions

It is early in the morning. Since my office faces right into the waiting room and my visibility allows me to see youngsters seated there, I immediately spy one gal who is not looking too pleased with life. Knowing that she is one of my clients, I get up from my seat, approach her and invite her in to talk.

She enters my office, shuts the door a little too loudly, sits down and immediately bursts into tears.

"What's wrong?" I ask her as I decide to sit down next to her, and not at my desk. I often do this so there will not be the barrier of a desk between us. It's hard enough for a kid to communicate without my adding a physical barrier.

Shelly looks up at me through teary eyes and tells me that she never wants to go home again. Listening patiently, she lets me know that she and her mom are not on the best of terms.

"She doesn't understand me and neither does John."

"Who is John?" I ask.

"He's (and that word is emphasized with a twinge of venom) my stepfather."

Aha...now we're getting somewhere. From our conversation, I find out that Mom has gotten married last summer after being divorced for seven years. During the previous seven years, she and Shelly had been very close, almost like sisters. They shared things, went places together, and confided in each other. Then, John had to enter the picture and everything changed!

"I hate her, Mrs. Cohen!" and with that the crying ensues.

I ask Shelly if I may call her mom. Note that Shelly is not blaming John; instead, she is choosing to blame the one she feels has betrayed her, her mother.

Later that morning, Mom enters my office. Knowing that Mom was coming in, Shelly already had returned to my office. When Mom sat down, Shelly pushed her own chair further away. Neither looked at the other. Both looked at me and I felt as it they were waiting for me to wave a magic wand.

Instead, I welcomed Mom and started to ask her some questions. She confirmed that Shelly and Mom had been very close. I asked what it was like now. She related to me that Shelly has become unruly, gets into trouble, and acts surly. Questioning her about when this behavior began, I was told that it just started last summer.

"What happened last summer?" I queried.

"John and I were married."

Through further conversation, it became apparent that Shelly felt Mom didn't care about her anymore. Instead, she saw Mom bestowing all her attention on John.

Looking intently at Mom I asked, "Do you tell Shelly you love her? Do you give her hugs? Do you still do things alone with her sometimes?"

Mom considered these questions and as she did, I watched Shelly squirm in her seat. Next, I watched Mom's eyes fill with tears. As she started to cry, so did Shelly. We talked some more and both realized that the dynamics of the house had changed, but that didn't mean that the feelings Mom and Shelly had for each other had to change, too.

Mom and Shelly decided that they would pick out one night to spend together, shopping, and eating out. Just the two of them. Both would try to be more open with the other by sharing thoughts, feelings and displays of endearment.

John, wishing to treat Shelly as one of his own, had started to be the disciplinarian. Naturally, Shelly took exception to this.

"Who does he think he is to tell me how to lead my life?"

Mom decided she would talk to John about this situation.

Through our talking, I think Mom and Shelly began to recognize some things. Mom was trying to be such a good wife to John that she had not noticed that she was neglecting Shelly and Shelly didn't feel comfortable sharing her feelings with Mom. Now both realized that change is not easy, but it can be handled if feelings are aired.

***

I Can't Believe He Left

Ed came into my office, shut the door and took a seat. He started to talk so quickly that I had trouble keeping up with his thoughts. His anger was palpable; his feelings were hurt. He felt bereft and was reaching for comfort.

It seems that Ed's dad came home one evening and announced to the family that he was leaving. No explanations were given except that he was unhappy. His three children were incredulous and his wife was dumbfounded. No one had seen this coming.

Ed was in my office searching for answers. Could he have done something wrong to get his father upset? What had his mom done? Should he be annoyed at her? What about his siblings? There seemed to be so many questions, yet there appeared to be no answers and the father's solution to separate was not the one that Ed wanted.

"I really hate him, Mrs. Cohen. He calls me at home and wants to take me out. Frankly, I don't want to see him or talk to him again."

"Ed," I say gently, "I can hear that you're angry. Your family all of a sudden is disintegrating and you feel powerless."

Looking at me, Ed responded, "And you know, the strange thing is, I am so upset with my dad, but I still love him and maybe that's why I hurt so much. I know. I'm so confused."

"You know," I continued, "It's okay to still love your dad. He's your dad and you have shared good times together. But it's okay, too, to dislike what he is doing to your family."

Ed thought for a moment and then nodded his head, yes. I continued to talk to him and pointed out that Dad's leaving was no reflection on Ed or his siblings. Clearly, it was a decision that Dad chose to make. Dad was not separating from Ed; he was separating from Ed's mother. Ed thought this over and felt a little relieved that he was not the reason behind Dad's obvious unhappiness.

"You know, Ed, by not going out with your dad, you are really giving him no opportunity to offer you any explanations. When he left, he probably felt he couldn't share anything. Now that some time has elapsed, he may feel able to shed some light on his decision, or he may not choose to do so. But, do go out with him, not to say okay to what he has done, but to keep the communication open, to listen to his side. Be honest with him. Tell him that you dislike his actions. You're angry and upset and he needs to see that, hear that, and deal with it. On the other hand, he is your dad and it is hard to just turn off that love. So keep the love, and make the date to see him. Anger and isolation solve nothing; meeting and sharing solve so much more."

**

Change Your Way of Thinking

Rumors

Hey, even just seeing the word makes my skin crawl. So many problems could be avoided if there were no rumors, but alas, that will never happen. It seems people thrive on them.

Take today for instance. Four girls were in my office; one was obviously heartbroken and the other three girls were present to give her support and to corroborate what she was going to tell me. Well, Stacy began her tale. You know the usual high school stuff. She said that she said that she said that she said that I had done such and such to so and so.

"And it's not true, Mrs. Cohen It's all a lie."

I countered with, "Then why do you think she said those things about you? Was any of it based in fact?"

After asking questions to hopefully shed light on the situation, I was able to ascertain that Stacy did own part of the problem. She had, in fact, done some things that may have seemed inappropriate. However, what she had done was told to one girl, then to another girl, and by the time it had finished making the rounds, most of what was being passed along was not based totally in fact. It had been embellished.

You know, if you want to tell a good story, you might as well enhance it here and there to make it that much more interesting. It's sort of like the old game called Telephone. The original message is passed along through different receivers and by the time it reaches the original sender, it has changed considerably and then what others perceive and hear is different from the reality of the situation.

Then, too, there is another problem. Only the message, albeit altered, is being heard. The whys and the wherefores are not accompanying it. Perhaps there is a good reason that such and such was done or said, but that reason is not shared. How different the action would look if it were couched in the appropriate setting. The person being talked about needs his or her day in court. That person needs a chance to explain.

I always find it so amazing how much backstabbing there is in high school. The perpetrator of the rumor usually has a reason...or so she thinks...to pass on the information about the other person. Usually I find the rumor is started because of jealousy. The girl is upset with Stacy, so why not pass on what she has heard about her, perhaps change it just a bit, and then Stacy will get hers. After all, she should suffer a little too. It's time to put her down a peg.

As I explained to Stacy, Meg (the assumed starter of the rumor) had been upset with Stacy since Stacy was presumably now dating the guy that Meg really liked, so how could Meg retaliate? Of course…spread a rumor, get the guy to think badly of Stacy or perhaps get others to think ill of her in order to get Stacy upset.

"You know what, Stacy? Meg's strategy is working. You are upset, and by your getting upset, you are letting Meg win. What would you like me to do?"

The three other gals all looked at her for a response and when none was forthcoming, I interjected, "Why don't we invite Meg to come into my office? Let's talk through this issue. Maybe Meg does not even realize how much she is hurting you. Maybe she was not the original starter of the rumor. Maybe when she heard the news, she was hurt and didn't think to check with you to see if the rumor were true or not. Or maybe, just maybe, Meg is feeling down and misery does love company, so she is trying to pull you down, too. What do you think? I mean there are a number of possibilities but we will never know which one is the right one unless we confront Meg. In fact, we will be enabling the rumor to continue."

Well, I did call Meg into my office. I had the other three girls go back to their classes. This issue was between Meg and Stacy so the others were not needed and besides, I felt that Stacy and Meg would have a better chance to air their feelings if it were just the two of them with me present as a facilitator.

I had one girl present her side of the story; then the other gal spoke. Then, we compared notes and saw how the rumor was only partially based in truth. The rest was hogwash. Once the situation was truthfully presented and clearly understood, Meg looked very apologetic.

And Meg had not started the rumor. She had simply kept it going because she had been so upset by what she had heard…so upset to think her good friend would have betrayed her. Her perception of the whole situation was so different from the reality. She had to change the way she had looked at things.

Then all three of us discussed rumors, the ugliness of them, the angst and the confusion they cause and what should now be done to deal with this one. We talked for about an hour. It was good; it was revealing; it was healing. We all grew from the experience. At the end of the session, both girls gave each other a hug. They had been close friends in the past and of course, that was why they had hurt even more when the rumor started flying.

"You know, gals, don't believe what you hear about someone else unless you hear it from that someone else and give that person a chance to explain."

I smiled, they smiled, and then together they left my office, ready to continue their day.

***

Did You Hear It From My Lips?

Sitting in my office, I watched the two angry girls clearly as they shot each other dagger looks and spoke accusatory words. Clearly, Jane was upset. She had heard rumors that were untrue and because of them she felt her friends had abandoned her. Carol, the supposed perpetrator of the rumors, kept interrupting Jane and denying that any malicious and untrue words had been said. But, the argument continued, the shouting increased, and name-calling ensued.

Like a referee, I finally made the time-out sign and told both girls it was now my turn and that I would brook no interference from either one until I called on each for her thoughts.

"Let's be civilized", I suggested. "Nothing will be gained from shouting; nothing will be heard and nothing will be settled. You will just cause each other to yell and your emotions will take over."

Through conversation, it became clear that Jane had, in fact, said some things to some of her friends and Carol had heard this and then told some other mutual friends. Jane didn't mean to say cruel things, but things were not going well at home and she had to vent somewhere and at someone. So, yes, she guessed she had used some nasty words, but then, too, she had told her friends to disregard what she had said because she was having a bad time.

"Wait!" I implored. "Regardless of a bad day or not, you still said the words, Jane; you still called them names. You still hurt their feelings. And you know why? I suggest that you were feeling so bad about yourself, that you wanted to knock your friends down a peg or two so they could share the same miserable place that you were in emotionally, so you called them names so they would feel hurt, like you."

Jane reluctantly said that maybe I was right but she still accused Carol of being mean by misconstruing her words and passing around rumors.

At this time, I watched Carol react and as she did, I decided to let her take the driver's seat for a while. Clearly she was revved up and wanted to have her say.

Pointing at Jane, Carol asked, "Did you see those words coming from my lips? Did you? Did you actually see me speaking them?"

Jane sort of moved back in her seat, she stared for a moment then responded, "No, but I heard you had said things."

"You heard, but you heard from others, not from me. Unless you actually hear something from me, don't believe it."

"That's a good point, Carol, and one so many of us forget," I said. "We should never assume something. You both know what that word, assume, means, don't you? It means to make an ass out of you and me and that's what happens when you assume anything. You must search out the truth; you must ask the person whom you know is involved. You must not be judgmental, but rather listen to all the facts."

Looking at Jane, I continued, "Jane, now you know that you did upset some of your friends, so they probably are annoyed at you, but you also know that Carol did not spread any rumors about you."

Next I looked at Carol. "Carol, now perhaps you have more of an understanding of why Jane has acted the way she has, not that that excuses Jane for her actions, but perhaps you might have some compassion."

Well, the girls continued to talk, but this time to and with each other, rather than at each other. I found I had to interject less and less and watched carefully and happily as they came to some sort of understanding. Then, I sent each back to her class. Another crisis averted!

But, once they had left, I realized how much I had gleaned from the confrontation. It is so important to look within yourself, to ascertain your motives, to see where they come from. It is necessary to search out the reality of the situation and change your way of looking at it.

It is important to be honest with yourself, to feel good about yourself and then you can be honest with others and won't have the desire to knock them down. I particularly will remember Carol's words, "Did you hear it from my lips? If not, don't believe it."

***

135

Perceptions

Today a young lady came into my office. Clearly, she was agitated. Her mother had called to discuss different issues that were occurring in school and at home.

As I spoke to the young lady, she shared with me that her parents don't really care about her. When she does something good, she never hears praise. Now that she has some problems, they have gotten on her case. When she was relating this to me, I could hear the undercurrent of anger. Her eyes were flashing, her lip was quivering and her hands were gesturing.

As we talked further, I asked her an important question. "If your parents do not care about you, then why did they bother to call me?"

She thought about this for a minute, but dismissed it and got back to her kick about their only butting in when she fails. I let her talk for a while to vent her emotions. Once I felt that she had let out a lot of her anger, we started talking about perceptions.

I explained to her that perceptions are assumptions; they are guesses about a situation. We are assuming that someone feels a certain way when in reality he may not. Therefore, it is very important to share our feelings, to let the person know about our perceptions. This allows the person to know where we are coming from and to challenge our way of feeling. In doing this, our perceptions will change and will be based on reality.

Perceptions are so often misleading. They are the roots of many arguments and hard feelings. Sometimes we look at a person, ask a question, and the response seems to be curt. Immediately, we may feel that person does not like us. WRONG! Maybe, the person is in a hurry, so she had to give us a quick response.

Two young men were quite upset by the death of a classmate. One dealt with it by crying openly; the other chose to yell and scream at someone, yet did not cry. Outwardly, an observer might feel that the one who was crying was grieving more keenly, yet, in this case, that was not true. The perception was clearly wrong.

In a classroom, a teacher yelled at a student to get down to business, to do his work. The student perceived that the teacher disliked him. Instead, the teacher truly liked the kid and wanted him to succeed.

Many times kids come in my office upset that a friend is angry with them or no longer likes them. Just as often, the perception is wrong. In reality, the friend was having a bad day or had an argument at home and was taking his/her feelings out on the other friend. Only through sharing this can the onlooker know the true feelings.

It is so important to separate perception from reality. It is important to not make snap judgments; instead, it is necessary to search for the real meaning behind overt actions and feelings and then to change our way of looking at things.

$$***$$

$P = I + E$

You're probably wondering if this guidance counselor is into physics or chemistry. I mean what's with the formula? You think pie is something that is eaten or else stands for 3.14. Yeah, well at times, but these letters stand for something a little different, and when you add the I and the E together, you get a person. So let's take a look at how this formula works.

According to Cohen (that's me), each person is comprised of two important parts, intellect and emotion. It's how these parts come together that will determine P, the person. Notice that I wrote $P = I + E$. That's because I feel that the intellect and the emotion should be utilized in equal parts in order to make the person function in the most beneficial and efficient way. Now let's take a look at the three letters in this formula and carefully examine each one.

I = intellect. What really separates us from the rest of the animal kingdom is the superior quality of our intellect. Yet, when a problem arises, how often do we tap into our intellect? Do we use it to its fullest? Once the situation is presented, do we examine it from all sides, do we listen to its proponents and opponents, do we research it, and then, and only then, do we come up with a solution? I think not. I think, instead, that we often let the E which = emotions take over and crowd out the intellect part, so no longer are the I and E in the equation equal. Then P = person is not acting in an appropriate manner.

Let's look at an example. Jimmy comes home with a really lousy report card. Usually a good student, he has earned mainly C's and D's. Clearly, you, as his parent, are very unhappy. You call in Jimmy to discuss the situation. After you ask him why he received those grades and he starts to offer an explanation, you interrupt him and start yelling. Your emotions have taken over; you are not even waiting to give him a chance to explain. Perhaps if you had, you would have found out that Jimmy was having a hard time socially in school, that his personal problems were usurping his powers of concentration. Then, upon hearing this, you would be able to intellectually figure out that yes, his grades would be adversely affected and yes, you now should try to work through some of his issues so that he will begin to get back down to the business of studying.

And that takes me to Jimmy. I said he has problems concentrating; he has lost his focus because of personal problems. What's happening with Jimmy's equation? It's gotten messed up; the I and the E are not equal. Jimmy is letting his emotions take over. He has to own the fact that his emotions are what are ruling him and until he works out his personal problems, he will not be able to look at his situation in an objective way.

Clearly, one can see what happens when emotions override intellect, but what happens when intellect overrides emotions? Let's look at Mrs. Smith, a teacher. A mother comes in to talk to her and tells her why Debbie is doing so poorly in school. It seems Mom and Dad are divorcing, brother has left for college, and Grandma has died. Hey, I could even add that their favorite pet has died, too, in order to really emphasize the trauma that Debbie is feeling. Well, Mrs. Smith listens, albeit unsympathetically, while mother finishes her story.

Then, Mrs. Smith says, "Yes, and your point is? You know Debbie should be able to separate her problems at home from issues here at school. Please tell your daughter to start concentrating!"

And so the story goes. The problem? Mrs. Smith is being ruled totally by her intellect. She must mix in some pathos, some understanding, and some emotionalism to better understand and deal effectively with the situation.

From these scenarios, I am sure you get my drift. It is so important to put into play both the I and the E in order to obtain a productive P. Search your mind, and search your heart in order to grapple with problems. Make sure you are viewing them realistically. Then and only then will you be able to deal with them wholly and be able to find viable solutions

***

Looking in the Rearview Mirror

Poor Jane. She had tried her best for the team, but unfortunately, she had made a big mistake and it had cost her and the team dearly. In a few days it would be her turn to play again and clearly she was concerned.

She told me that she just couldn't get the picture out of her mind that she had made a mistake. Try as she might she couldn't let it go. Her teammates and coach were cool; after all, it had been a team effort and if they had all hung in there better, perhaps they could have won. So they did not blame Jane. But that didn't seem to make a difference.

I asked Jane if she drove. She shook her head yes. Then I asked when she used the rearview mirror. Of course, she looked at me in surprise, wondering why I was asking. But, she answered my question. It turned out that she used it to see what was behind her, and then she would look ahead in order to continue her driving.

"Yes, how right you are…and that's what you have to do in life, too, Jane. It is important to remember for a moment what is behind you, but then you must forge ahead. If you chose to just look in the rearview mirror, you would never get anything accomplished. You would be stuck with what's behind you and never be able to move forward. You know it is important to glance backwards every once in a while to see where you have been and to learn from the past. After all, we do not want to repeat past mistakes. However, once that has been done, it is important to let go of the past in order to move along."

Jane thought over what I was saying and after some discussion I said, "Jane, what benefit is there to keep dwelling on your mistake? Are you going to be able to change it? If you keep thinking about it, will it help you focus on the next game you play in or will it hamper your concentration?"

Like with Jane, as we go through life, we will all make mistakes. When we do, it is important to recognize the mistakes, to look at them, to learn from them, but then to let them go. We must let them go if we are to continue to get on with our lives. Otherwise we will be stuck in our yesterdays and never truly enjoy today. So much energy will be used on musing about the past, that we will have nothing left to help us grapple with the present in order to positively affect the future.

Not only will we perhaps be stuck in the past, but also we will not be able to perform our best in the present. Our vision will not be clear; instead, it will be clouded over with past images. Our perceptions of the current situation will not match the reality. In our minds our error or whatever the situation was will increase in intensity often making the situation seem worse than it was.

If we are made to dwell on the past, more than likely we will be so uptight, depressed, and unfocussed that some past issues may be repeated and in that case, the past will become part of the present.

So it is necessary to change our focus and to look at what is occurring now, for it is the present that will lead us into the future.

***

Change is Scary

Are you fed up with certain things …perhaps your daily routine…and you've considered a change? You complain about your circumstances, look into alternatives, but then just go back to what you've been doing. Why? If things are so uncomfortable, if things make you so unhappy, then why do you continue doing what you are doing? With a resounding answer, I can tell you in one word, CHANGE!!!!

Believe it or not, what you are currently doing has put you in a comfort zone. Whether it causes you to feel good or not, you are familiar with it and even comfortable with your discontent. It has become a part of you, so even though you seek change, you sort of tell yourself that "the devil you know is better than the devil you don't know". In other words, you decide to put up with what you have. You continue to feel frustrated, you reconsider change, and then you stay where you are. And so it continues…

This can be related to everyone, adults and kids. Kids don't like when a new year starts; they have new teachers and that means change. New kids are in their classes and that means change. And change is threatening. It drags along with it the unknown and the unknown is something you have not tried before, so it fills you with anxiety.

Change takes guts. Yet, people I know who have embraced change have grown from the experience. They feel rejuvenated, jump-started, and refreshed. The boredom has disappeared and has been replaced by challenge and opportunity. They no longer feel stagnant

Think about a pool. Unless new chemicals are put into the water, it does become stagnant. Similarly, unless we embrace new ideas and new experiences, we become stagnant which causes frustration and even anger and depression.

Okay, so let's say you're one of the gutsy ones and you've decided to change. You take on the new things and ask yourself, "Why did I change? This isn't so great!" Stop yourself. Remember why you did change. The other was not great and this can be with time. After all, you have to get used to something new.

I think back to when so many youngsters stormed my office, voicing their unhappiness with their teachers. I told them to come see me again in a week, but only after immersing themselves in their classes, and having a positive mental outlook. When the week ended and they returned, many no longer complained about their teachers. They had become accustomed to them. Actually, some were enjoying their teachers' new methods, compared to the methods they had experienced last year.

Next time you feel down and out, next time you think you might want to try something new, weigh what you have, why you want to change, and what the change will offer you. If the scales dip in favor toward the change, go for it! I can almost guarantee you that you will be glad you did!

Chance new things
Have a positive attitude
Apply yourself
New things take time
Growth comes from change
Enjoy your new opportunity

***

A Geographical Cure

How many times have you thought that if you could only change your surroundings things would definitely improve?

But will that really work? Think about yourself as a person. You have your outward physical part and then you have your inner workings …the part that is hidden deep inside, the emotions, the wants, the desires, the foibles, the disappointments, the depression, the elation, etc. We can't see these things, but we know they exist.

They are separate from the part that the onlooker sees. They are always there and direct who we are and how we act. No matter where we move physically, our thoughts and feelings are always with us.

Jerry came into my office. We were talking about his difficult home life and his impending graduation. From there we talked about his plans for the future.

"You know, Mrs. Cohen, I just want to get as far away from here as I can get. I want to leave all this junk behind and start out fresh. I want to go some place where no one will know me and no one will know my background."

"Do you really think that is possible to do?" I countered. "You know, Jerry, wherever you go you will be taking yourself along... your inner self. You can't get rid of that. You might be trying for a geographical cure, but that's just what it will be. You will be in a different place, but you will still be you. Do you get what I mean?"

"Sort of," came the quiet reply.

I could tell he was musing about what I had just said. Our conversation continued and I explained to him that he would still have the same feelings, the same hopes, the same despair, and the same desires. What he had to learn to do was to change those things, to learn to look at things differently, to put them out where he could see them, to work them through, and then to go on. If he couldn't do that, it would not matter if he moved to China; he would still be the same Jerry. So geographically, he would be in a different place, but emotionally he would be the same.

I suggested to Jerry that he should write down all the things that are bugging him and see if he could look at them and deal with them differently. Moving to a new location was fine, but he had to change his inner workings, not just his physical location. After all, situations and problems would arise when he moved and he would have to deal with them. If he hadn't been able to change his attitude, etc., then he would be dealing with problems in the same manner as he has always done regardless of the fact that he has moved. A geographical cure will not work.

So many times we look for cures. We look to change teachers, to change spouses, to change how we dress, to change friends, but the bottom line usually is that we have to change ourselves...and then the cure, the search for happiness, will be in our reach.

***

Scholastic Success

School is Open

It is so hard to get back into the swing of things when school opens. When you think about it, school goes along at a frenzied pace, then it comes to a complete stop with summer only to become completely hectic again in the fall. There really is no in-between and I think that's what makes it so difficult when school resumes after the hazy, lazy days of summer. Instead of being able to rev the motor for a while, it definitely is full throttle from the beginning.

So, if I, the guidance counselor, feel this way, you can imagine how your children must feel. Not only are they going at full steam, but also they have to deal with new teachers, new classes, making or not making a sports team, missing a friend who was in school last year, getting accustomed to new faces, etc., etc., etc.

What can you as a parent do? Keep your cool. Many times your children will come home frustrated and out of sorts. If they seem to jump at a suggestion, or be unnecessarily grouchy, instead of reacting in like manner, sit down with your children. Speak to them quietly. As your voice lowers, so will theirs. Ask about their day. Remember, what may seem trivial to you does not appear trivial to them. Listen. Be understanding. Then, try to work out a solution to the apparent problem.

Most times children simply feel overwhelmed and they just don't have the coping skills to look calmly at things. Try to help them get organized.

1. Do they have a desk with proper lighting, pencils, paper, etc.?

2. Do they have an agenda, an assignment book?

3. Do they have a regular time set aside for studying?

4. Do they have a dictionary?

5. Do they have a quiet place to study?

6. Do they talk on the phone, listen to the radio, or have other diversions while they should be studying?

7. Do they arrange their assignments so that they complete the more difficult ones first?

8. Do they plan their time accordingly, so that they are not tackling their homework when they are exhausted?

9. Do they leave some time for leisure?

10. Do they feel comfortable asking you for help and having you quiz them?

11. Do they stay after school when they don't understand the material?

Show your children that you are interested in what they are doing. By your questions and interest, they will see that you care and that you feel that school is important. They will take their lead from you and share your feelings. They will take ownership of their problems, knowing that someone is there to help sort them out.

***

Adjustments

It is just amazing how many adjustments students have to make during a school year. They have enjoyed the summer, they have done their own thing, and now all of a sudden, they are thrust into a flurry of activity with bells ringing, deadlines that they have to meet, new faces, and new subjects. To say they have to adjust is an understatement! Their whole comfort zone has been upset and they find themselves in uncharted waters. How can they stay afloat?

The other day, a very beleaguered young man stood in my door.

"Mrs. Cohen," he lamented, "I am going to fail. I can't possibly take that English course. The teacher is so hard, the workload is impossible and I know I am going to flunk. Please get me out of it!"

"Well", I responded, "Just take a few deep breaths and let's discuss this in a calm fashion."

I needed to have him settle down. In an agitated condition, he could not possibly think logically. Well, together we discussed the class. I pointed out to him that he had only been in it for a few days. How could he really tell what the class was like? How could he really tell what the teacher was like? Yes, perhaps the workload initially seemed tough, but how did he really know until he started to tackle all the assignments. Then, too, not all the assignments were due at one time. The teacher had given them a syllabus for the term, not for the week!

He thought about what I had said and I continued. "You know, you have to adjust your thinking. If you take on a defeatist attitude, you will not make it. Think positively. I know you can do it."

And so the conversation continued. I have not called him back into my office; however, he has not asked to see me, so things must be improving. He must have adjusted his thinking.

I still remember the young lady who came in last year and just had to get out of her science class or she would just die…I mean like she just couldn't exist!!! Well, she stayed in that class; after all, she had signed up for it and I knew she could and should handle it. Initially, she was not happy but about a month later the same young lady came into my office and told me how much she loved her science class, her teacher was great and she was learning so much. Yes, she had adjusted. She had settled in and now she was able to cope, to learn, and even to enjoy.

Not only do students have to adjust their thinking in regard to teachers and assignments, but also they must adjust their daily routine. It is important to make a schedule and to try to stick to it. In the summer, time had no real meaning. Now it means everything. What to do?

They have to make out a schedule, keeping their priorities straight. Yes, talking on the phone, television, and just hanging out are important, but they should not take top priority. Homework must and should come first. Then, there will be ample time for fun. If there is not time today, then there will be time tomorrow. The main thing is not to let themselves feel overwhelmed. They should assess what they have to do, and then tackle the tasks one at a time. Initially, what seems impossible will become possible with time.

And what about friends? There, adjustments have to be made, too. Interests change and with that friends change, too. It is important for students to seek out friends with whom they feel comfortable. They have to realize that they may have to adjust their thinking; they may disagree with some of their friends' ideas and that's okay, but they have to remember not to be too judgmental. Each person is an individual with unique thoughts and actions. Recognize that and if the student can adjust to that, then the friendship should continue. If not, then perhaps it is time to make new friends.

Adjustments are not easy. They involve change, but remember, with change, comes growth and that's what high school is all about. It provides students with the opportunity to mature. It necessitates their learning coping skills that will enable them to flourish.

***

Not Just Santa Claus Should Make Lists

I have to tell you, I am really a disorganized person, but somehow out of the chaos that usually existed on my desk, now I have been able to find things and know what needs to be done. It's truly amazing, but I can! However, I must tell you, it hasn't always been that way. What saved me? My husband. He is so neat that I am afraid to have anything lying around since he will simply pick it up and place it in an orderly pile.

His office looks sterile…as if no one works in there. That neatness has not totally rubbed off on me, but what I have learned from him is to make lists. And I must tell you, those precious lists have helped me immeasurably.

The usual list is a grocery list, but I have found that lists work for everything, and the older I get, the more essential they become. They are my crutch for remembering. When I come home, and there are messages on my answering machine, I write them down, I make a list, and then I return the calls.

When I have a myriad of chores to do, I write them down, and then prioritize them. As I complete each task, I cross it off the list. And so it goes. I find that a pencil and paper exist in most rooms so I can jot something down when it comes to mind.

Now that I have mastered list making, I have passed it on to my students. I tell them to write down their assignments. As they think of different tasks that they have to do during the day, they should make note of them, too. Then, when they arrive home, they should reorganize their lists, giving top priority to the tasks that must be accomplished soon. It's amazing, but just sequencing the jobs helps you to organize your thinking and to proceed in a more orderly fashion.

To remember items on a test, it is good to make lists and then try to make a mnemonic device using the points you have written down. An example may be the Great Lakes. Think of their names and that there are 5. Then take the first letter of each lake and try to make those letters into a word. H-Huron, O-Ontario, M-Michigan, E-Erie, S-Superior and voila, you have the word HOMES. Now all you have to do is think of the word HOMES and the names of the lakes will come easily to you.

You know, it's good to make lists for more than one day. A matter of fact, I usually make them for the week. That way, I get an overview of all the tasks I wish to complete and then can pace myself during the next seven days. And if I really work it out in the best possible way, I can sometimes have the weekend all to myself, but that rarely happens.

Once your lists are made, leave space to add more items, since one task will probably lead to another and you will have to add things. The lists will not only organize you, but also will make you realize how much you have accomplished.

So, don't leave the list making to Santa Claus. Become a list maker yourself and you will be delighted with the results. I know I am, but I do hate to tell my husband he's right!

***

It Takes Guts to be Imperfect

Many of the problems that we see in our students today stem from the fact that some of them feel they have to be perfect and that is a very tall order!

Unfortunately, perfectionists can never really attain their goal of perfection. Think about it for a minute. Is anything perfect? No. So a perfectionist can never truly be happy. She can try and try but never reach self-satisfaction because nothing is ever perfect enough.

Working with these youngsters can be very challenging. We want students to try to do their best, so how do we tell them not to be such perfectionists? First, we must define perfection as absolutely perfect, and then relate to them that there is nothing on this earth that is absolutely perfect.

If we look at a piece of furniture, there is certain to be a nick or a scratch. Maybe there is a blemish on an otherwise white piece of paper, or perhaps one of the flowers planted in a row grows just a little taller than all the other flowers. And the list goes on. It's important to realize that although people and things are not perfect, it is the imperfections that make life more interesting. After all, it would be so dull if everything were perfect and the same.

Perfectionists dwell on their mistakes. They don't see the entire passage that they wrote; they only see the red marks on the paper. Dwelling on mistakes saps their energy and takes away their pleasure. They can never truly be happy with what they have accomplished.

Kim came into my office. She was getting headaches, feeling very tense and finding that she would cry easily. We started discussing what could be bothering her. She related to me that she had always done well in school, but this year, her junior year, seemed to be so different. Yes, she was taking advanced courses, but she felt she could handle them when she signed up for them. But now, she is having trouble. Of course, I found out that trouble to Kim meant that she is earning B's, not A's.

We looked at this. Through further discussion, it came out loud and clear that Kim is a perfectionist. Everything has to be just right or why bother doing it at all? I told her it was okay to get B's; it was okay not to get an A. I felt she had to redefine her idea of excelling. Excelling does not mean perfection. Excelling means to do one's best in what one is undertaking.

"Do you feel you are achieving to your capacity?"

Kim thought about this and decided she was. In fact, she could not work any harder.

"Okay, then Kim, you are doing as well as you can and that is good. You are excelling. You know, it's important to work your hardest, but don't work for perfection. You can never reach it. No one can ever reach it. Instead, work to do your best. Kim, it will take guts for you to be imperfect, but being imperfect will allow you to tackle new things without fear of failure and to be pleased with what you are doing. I bet your headaches and tension will lessen, too."

I continued by telling her that no one wears earned grades around her neck. She listened, she responded, she seemed relieved. Then, I added that some colleges have addressed the issue of perfection by allowing kids to take some courses Pass/Fail. Others do not record a grade if a student fails; rather the school allows the person to retake the course or to take a different one.

As parents and teachers we can help these perfectionists by example. If we make a mistake, it is important to admit it. We need to give students permission to be imperfect, to take pride in doing the best that they can do socially, athletically, and academically. Often, they will be surprised. If they do not consciously strive for perfection, they may even do better than they had done before since they will not be so uptight. Without reaching for perfection, they will find that they do excel.

***

"Out-Scheduled"?

When Jim walked into my office, I felt tired! His obvious fatigue was contagious. With his head hung down, his shoulders slumped, and his feet dragging, Jim did not look the picture of health. He took a seat and we started talking. As he looked up, I could see dark circles under his eyes.

"Jim," I asked with concern, "Is something troubling you? To tell you the truth, you really don't look too good. A matter of fact, you look exhausted. What's the deal?"

And then, slowly his story unfolded.

Jim told me that the family was going through some hard times. Dad had been laid off; money was very tight. There were a lot of mouths to feed and even with Mom working, it just didn't compute. He decided to help out by taking a job. In itself, that was a laudable idea, but I queried how many hours he worked. He told me that he works on the weekends and three days a week.

"Jim, no wonder you're exhausted. I know you play sports and are talking a very difficult course load in school. How can you possibly have time for everything? Making money is good and I applaud you for helping out the family, but if you don't get enough sleep and then get sick, whom will you be helping?"

I reached over and took out a sheet of paper.

"Jim, write out your schedule. What hours do you do things? Let's see it all on paper and then we'll be able to deal with it."

Jim took the paper and wrote out his schedule. It looked something like this.

6:45AM – awaken and get ready for school

7:05AM – go to school

2:00PM – leave school for practice

5:30 – 10PM – work

10:30PM – get home

10:30-12PM – do homework

I looked at the schedule with him and asked him when he finds time to eat? He really doesn't! It seems he lives on snack food. Then, we talked about homework. If he does it that late at night, how completely and accurately is it done? How many hours does he sleep? Then, when we examined the little time he has to get ready for school, he realized why he feels so rushed and often forgets to bring school materials with him.

Looking at him, I naturally said, "Jim, your schedule has to change. You are packing too much in with hardly any time for sleeping and eating. No wonder you're exhausted! Let's see what we can do to make this schedule workable."

We decided to prioritize things. His grades are important. Since Jim is a very intelligent young man, he wishes to further his education, and especially now with money so tight, getting good grades will help him get a scholarship. He excels in the sport he's playing and that could be an added hook that he needs for college acceptance and a scholarship. So, it became apparent that more time had to be allotted for homework, but we couldn't cut into his involvement with sports. Therefore, that left us with his job. He had to work, but perhaps he could rearrange his hours.

"Mrs. Cohen, I just started the job; what if they fire me because I can't work so many hours?" he asked with concern.

Picking up the phone, I said, "Well, you can always get another job. Besides, you don't know what the boss will say unless you ask him, so here, give him a call. Maybe he is there now."

Jim dialed the number and spoke to his boss, telling him that he needed to work, but he just couldn't do all the hours. Fortunately for Jim, the boss was amenable to his request for fewer hours and was able to rearrange things and keep Jim on. I remember the relief I saw in Jim's eyes after he hung up the phone.

Jim was able to change his schedule, to be in control of it without his schedule controlling him and that gave him a positive feeling. I saw him a week later and he was a different young man. His grades were improving, he was doing better on his team, and yes, even the rings under his eyes were lessening. Now, he was no longer "out-scheduled".

You know, as parents, it's important to sit down with your children and to make out a schedule. Not only does this help them to organize their time, but also it enables you to see if they are trying to do too many things. Besides, it's a good way to communicate and do some bonding.

***

Progress Reports

Yes, it's that time of year again when you hear the door quietly close followed by the sound of feet quickly going up the stairs. Or, your youngster comes home, greets you with a weird smile and is exceptionally nice to you! Yes, it's progress report time.

Just the thought sends chills through a parent. Is she failing anything, what did we do wrong, will he ever graduate? Well, take a deep breath. The sky is not falling and Lindsay still has the chance of doing very well.

First, ask your child for the progress reports. If they are not forthcoming and you feel they should be, please call your child's school. Counselors will be able to access them for you. Next, have a talk with your youngster. Some of the report may look good; other parts of it may look bad. Our school includes comments for all subjects; other schools choose to send home just warnings.

Find out the reasons behind the negative reports. Listen carefully, but realize, too, that you are just getting one side of the story, a side that will try to exonerate your daughter.

Don't waste your breath saying, "Unless you shape up, you'll never get into college; you'll never graduate from high school; you'll stay back!"

She knows that. Instead, simply inform your youngster that there will be a supervised homework time when phone calls will not be accepted, radios will not be blared, and televisions will not be watched.

Ask your child to keep an assignment book. Each night check to make sure that all assignments ARE being done. If your child has difficulty doing them, you will know and can call the school to find an appropriate tutor.

Call the school to set up weekly progress reports. Relate to your brooding youngster that these reports are not a punishment; rather they will let you both know what is happening in class. When they are all good, they will be stopped. If

152

you wish, you may also set up appointments with teachers. Make sure your child is present at the appointments. After all, it is about her. It's amazing, but with the student and the teacher present, a really true picture of the difficulty emerges.

By taking an active role in dealing with your child's progress reports, you are sending her the message that you really care. You are saying in effect, "Together, we will deal with this. I am here to help you."

***

Talk the Talk or Walk the Walk

How many times have people told you that they are going to do something, but then it never seems to happen? They talk about it and discuss it but then they never seem to put into action what they have said. In other words, they are talking the talk, but not walking the walk.

I still remember Joe who would come into my office and not under his own volition. Every time the marking term would end or progress reports would come out, it was necessary for me to call Joe and strongly urge him to come in to talk to me. Naturally, we would discuss the dismal grades that he was earning. He would listen, then look at me and give me a million reasons why his grades were that way. Usually, the reasons concerned someone else or something else that had adversely affected Joe and therefore his grades. He would promise me that this term none of those things would be in his face; he would apply himself and his grades would soar.

"Just watch, Mrs. Cohen, I know this term will be different. I know I'll do the work."

Well, you guessed it. The grades would be the same and so would the conversation in my office.

Finally, I tried a different approach.

"Joe, you tell me all the things you're going to do, but you never seem to do them. You know, it's sort of like getting all your things packed in a suitcase and then not taking the trip, or maybe it's like talking about the trip you're going to take, but then never actually taking it. You know, Joe, you talk the talk, but you never seem to walk the walk."

"Yeah, I guess you're right, but why do I do that?"

153

We talked for a while and I tried to get him to think why. We decided that it's so much easier to just talk about something rather than to actually do it. Doing it takes a lot more work. Then, too, when you talk about it, you sort of convince yourself that you've dealt with it when in actuality you haven't.

I suggested to Joe that he write down what he says regarding how he will bring up his grades and change those things that are interfering with his success. By writing them down, he will be able to look at them, and check each off as he deals with each item. In this way, he will be walking the walk; he will be doing each thing that will take him closer to his final destination – success. I told him to make certain that he stops after he completes each thing and reassesses how he is doing. Then, he may proceed.

Yes, the road may be bumpy at times, he may hit some detours, but if he really wants to finish his journey, he will.

"You know, Joe," I said, looking at him earnestly, "You must have a plan, a desire and diligence to carry it off; otherwise, you will just talk the talk and not walk the walk."

***

The ABC's of Learning

After giving some thought to how to succeed in high school, I have come up with an ABC plan for success and want to share it with you so you will, in turn, share it with your children.

A stands for attitude. It is so important for your child to have a good attitude about himself, others and school in general. If he has a negative attitude, then everything around him will appear negative. He will not want to enter into activities, get involved in his schoolwork, or perhaps even go to his classes. Instead, he will prefer to just "veg out". But if his attitude is a positive one, his glass will definitely appear to be at least half full; he will welcome going to school, meeting with his friends, joining groups and just enjoying life. With a happy disposition, he will positively affect those around him, too, which will aid in his own sense of well-being.

A stands for agenda. The student should have an agenda at the beginning of the school year; it allows him to record his assignments in an orderly fashion. It is essential for him to keep his agenda up to date and to refer to it often. As parents, you should ask to see his agenda, not only to show that you are interested in what he is doing in school, but also to make certain that he is completing his assignments. As he fulfills each assignment, he should cross it off. If he has a question about it, he should write that down in the agenda and then ask the teacher about it the following day.

B stands for books. Books help tell a story. Teachers elaborate on the books, or maybe it's vice-a-versa, but both are essential to learning. A child should read his assignments before class, and then make sure he takes notes on the important facts. It's good to look at the bold headings; these point out what the chapter is about and provide a good method by which a child can quiz himself. He should look at each heading and see if he can answer vital points about it. As he reads, he should take notes on his reading. Never just skip over the pictures; these are important and the visual images may help him to remember different facts. If he doesn't understand what he is reading, he should make a note of what he is confused about and question the teacher about it. He should keep up with his reading, carry his book to class, and refer to it as necessary.

B stands for behavior. If your child is not paying attention to the task at hand, if he is fooling around with others, or trying to gain attention through silly antics, he will not be able to learn essential material. How can he? He won't hear it and not hearing it will preclude his understanding it when he has to do some examples at home. He should strive to pay attention. If another child is bothering him, he should ask to have his seat changed.

C stands for classroom and communication. It's in the classroom where so much of the learning takes place so it is important for a youngster to attend class on a regular and timely basis. If he is late, he will miss important messages that the teacher will be imparting; maybe instructions will be voiced to explain assignments, or maybe a test will be given. If the student finds he must miss class, it is up to him to find out what work he will have missed and when he can make it up.

C stands for communication. Not only does the student have to listen in class, but also he should ask questions and volunteer answers. If he does not understand what the teacher is saying, he should ask questions. In addition, he should take clear and concise notes on every important point that is being made in class. When he goes home, he should review his notes and fill in the gaps by writing down what he has learned, but not recorded. When he studies for a test, he can form a study group with other students in the class and communicate with them prior to the test. In this way, each in the group can help the other learn material and reinforce his understanding.

These ABC's of learning are so important. If they are followed completely, the student will be organized, attend class regularly, read his assignments, ask and answer questions, and earn grades that are commensurate with his ability.

***

What Part of the Word Study Don't You Understand?

I had a young man in my office and finally asked him the above question. It seems that he took a zero on a paper because he just didn't have the time to do it.

Pondering this for a moment, incredulously I asked, "Why?"

The response was that his parents insisted he go to watch his younger siblings play sports.

"Really?" I continued in the same incredulous tone.

Well, he finally came clean and told me that he wanted to go to the games, wanted to hang out with his friends, wanted, it seems, to do just about everything except STUDY!! Of course, I can understand that, but the consequences are not what I would choose. Now, we both got down to the "nitty gritty" and started to discuss priorities and studying.

The word study just did not seem to be entrenched in his vocabulary. I informed him that whatever we do in life, we really have to practice in order to perfect it. We talked about the Olympics and I pointed out how assiduously the athletes had to work at perfecting their skills and then to keep trying to improve them even further. Actually, I informed him, they practice for hours at a time in order to compete for just a few minutes.

"They," I told him, "have the desire to achieve, the desire to win and that's what you must develop in order to be a successful student, a student who studies."

You know, it's true, if you have no desire to succeed, then why on earth would you put in time to accomplish success?

From our conversation, I found out that Joe wants to become an accountant. I took out some books in my office and went on the computer in order to show him the education that is needed to fulfill his dream. Now, he began to see the

156

light; he needed good grades to get into a good college and in order to succeed scholastically, he would have to study.

Okay, so what does one have to do in order to study? I laid out a plan for him. I told him that he needs a place with a desk, a chair, a good light, and relative quiet. He must use this place each time he studies. This place will spell study for him. Also, he should set aside the same time of day in order to do his studying. Sometimes he will have to juggle the time, but mostly he should keep to his schedule and in this way, his time for studying will become a habit.

During school, he should have a notebook in which he lists all his homework assignments. Then, he can cross out assignments as they are completed.

Now, how should he study? I suggested to him that he should tackle his difficult subjects first while his mind is still fresh. For most youngsters, I find they should get up and move about after one hour; otherwise, they will get antsy and brain drain will set in. He should review his notes, using a highlighter for important facts. He should review his book, doing active reading. In other words, he should ask himself questions about the topic as he reads. He should turn around the headings and make them into questions. Can he answer them? If he is confused, he should call a friend and/or make sure he writes down his concerns and shares them with the teacher in the morning.

I continued by telling him not to let himself get bogged down. He should study each night and should always spend a few minutes reviewing before he goes on to something new. If he seeks help the next day and is still confused, he should set up a time to talk further with the teacher, perhaps study with a friend, and/or seek out someone to tutor him. It is important not to get discouraged, but to keep plowing ahead!

With new vocabulary words in any subject, I strongly suggested that he make flash cards, join them together with a ring, and then keep reviewing them. Many times a youngster will learn something for the moment, feel he has mastered it for the test, and then promptly forget it when the test is over. Therefore, by reviewing, he is reinforcing the material and really embedding it in his mind. I suggested, too, that he recite things aloud so that his sense of hearing will be involved, too. Many times it helps for a parent to review with him. The parent can leaf through the book and ask questions; he can quiz his child on vocabulary.

When he receives quizzes that he has taken, he should review his mistakes so he will not make the same mistakes the next time. He should keep all his quizzes and tests in a notebook and use them to review for his midterm and final exams.

Also, if a teacher records the wrong grade for one of the student's tests, the student will have the test to show the teacher.

From our meeting, Joe learned that studying is not an easy process, but it can be learned and done effectively and when it is, understanding ensues and grades soar. Self-esteem rises, too.

Hopefully, asking Joe the question, "What part of the word STUDY don't you understand?" now will be an inappropriate question. With his interest in learning, his parents' involvement, his friends' help and his teachers' input, Joe should be able to reach his potential and make his appropriate dreams into realities.

***

Who Is Fooling Whom?

Progress reports have been issued; they are the reports that notify the kids and their parents how they are doing. As counselors, we receive a copy. I look through them, highlight the kids who are really in trouble, and call them down so we can chat.

"Well, John, I see that you have received a few comments that show me you are not doing well in several classes. What seems to be the matter?"

John hems and haws, probably searching for a response that I will buy. Then he says, "Well, my parents won't let me use the computer and everything has to be typed."

"Please, John," I retort. "They won't let you use the computer? Even if you tell them you have to type stuff out in order to pass?"

He finally shares with me that some disrespectful actions have precluded his computer use.

"So," I continue, "then let's look at some options. Writing things out long hand isn't one of them. You can go into the library, you can stay after school, or you can use a friend's computer. Also, you can talk to your parents; perhaps make a contract about cleaning up your act. I mean there are things you can do."

That's just one scenario of why warnings or progress report were received. Others involve working late, but then come to find out the person is working so hard because he needs to pay for his truck. Or maybe another one tells me the teacher is so boring. And so the list of excuses goes on.

It's interesting, isn't it, that not many tell me that they just don't study for the tests. Not many tell me that they just don't go in for extra help. Not many tell me that they rarely take their books home. Not many tell me that they choose to study in the library because it is too noisy at home.

And then, sometimes when I do have a talk with a parent, and this is not true for all parents, and I suggest that progress reports be put into play, they will say, "Yeah, but don't do that yet. I don't want to pressure Susie too much. I will just talk to her; you know she is so busy and she does tell me that her teacher talks in a monotone and is so boring."

Now, who is making excuses for whom? Amazing, eh? But, I'm sure I've been that route, too. It just can't be totally my little darling's fault, but maybe I should look again. Maybe I should rethink how I feel. Maybe I should make an appointment with the teacher. Maybe I should call the guidance counselor. Maybe I should make compulsory study times. Maybe I should make sure that telephone calls are limited, television is limited, and instant messaging is limited. Maybe I need to be the one to set some boundaries. I am the adult; my son is the child.

Once some things have been put into play, it is important to monitor your child. It's important to make sure he is buying into everything; it is important to make sure that he wishes to achieve. Without the desire, all the boundaries that you put in place will not make a difference. Try to get your child to understand the importance of an education. Don't be too preachy or he will shut you out, but don't be afraid to share your thoughts either. That's the only way he will learn how you feel. But I do stress that your child must want to improve or all the urging in the world will not make him change.

It's time for him to take ownership of his grades. It's time for him to stop making excuses since excuses allow him to forgive himself and once he does that, there is no reason to change.

Therefore, consider…who is fooling whom?

***

Will You Keep the Ship Afloat?

Jerry was summoned to my office. I was very upset after his mother had visited with me and shared the unsettling news that Jerry was planning to drop out of high school, something that was clearly unacceptable to her or her husband.

"Please help us, Mrs. Cohen," she implored. "We have six children, all adults now, and only one has seen high school through to graduation. I keep telling Jerry that times are different now. It is so essential to get a high school degree. His siblings are much older and it wasn't that way back then."

I took out a copy of Jerry's report card. Although the grades were nothing to write home about, Jerry was still in the running. He could pass all his subjects if he would come to class, do his work, and study for his tests. But, and this was a big but, he had to want to pass.

As Jerry sat across from me, I could tell that he was feeling a little uneasy as I took out his report card and discussed it with him

I finally asked the all-important question, "Jerry, what do you want to do? Do you want to graduate from high school or do you have other plans in mind?"

Looking up at me, Jerry replied, "I really don't like school. I think I'd like to drop out and find a job."

We then began to discuss what kind of work he could find without a diploma and would he be happy in that type of work. He wasn't sure, but he figured that it was a start.

I looked at the length of my desk and told him to imagine that it was his life. I then put my finger against the desk measuring off where I thought about 17 years would be.

"Jerry, this is where you are now. You have all the rest of this desk, this life of yours, to live. Putting in one more year at high school will only take up just a little more space, but what a difference it will make to the space that is left, to the rest of your life."

Jerry thought about this, but wasn't convinced. What more could I say, I wondered. Then another thought came into my mind...a ship in the middle of the ocean. I knew Jerry liked to sail so I thought perhaps he could relate to the analogy I was about to make.

I told him to envision that he was the captain of a ship that had sprung a few leaks. There were many people on his ship relying on him and his ability. What would he choose to do? Seemingly, without too much thought, he told me he would plug up the holes. Aha! That was just the answer I had wanted.

"Yes, Jerry, you would react, try to do everything possible to save the ship from sinking, and then take the ship and all those to shore who had been counting on you."

I told him that he, now, was like the sinking ship. He could choose to stay in school and graduate or he could choose to leave and the ship would just sink. But, there was precious cargo involved…his folks, his siblings, and the most important of all, Jerry.

Haltingly…not too sure of his decision, he said, "Well, I guess I could give it a try."

Together, we mapped out a plan. Jerry would meet with each teacher and figure out exactly what he needed to pass. He would then proceed to make up the work he had missed, study for the tests and try his hardest to succeed.

The task wasn't easy, but the stakes were high and Jerry was well worth the effort. Letting the ship sink was easy, but being able to plug in the holes, float, and reach shore would be so much more beneficial.

Thankfully, Jerry has chosen to keep his ship afloat and looks forward to reaching shore as he crosses the stage to get his diploma at graduation.

***

College Picking Time

Ah, that crisp fall air, the crunch of leaves as you walk, the shortened days, yes, fall has arrived. Apple picking has arrived and for high school seniors, college picking has arrived. The selection is bountiful; the choices may be difficult. There are many different variables to consider.

In order to do this, it is good to make a chart. Along the side of the chart, write the following: Size; Location; SAT Scores; Grade Point Average; Application Deadline; Fees; Essay; Financial Aid; Recommendations; Majors; Sports and/or anything else that you deem important. Then, along the top write in the various colleges that interest you. Once you have filled in the appropriate information, you will have a handy guide to look at, one that will allow you to see at a glance what you must do in order to fulfill the necessary requirements to apply to each school. In addition, you will be better able to compare one school to the next.

Size...how big is the college? If it is very large, will you feel lost? Will there be teaching assistants rather than professors teaching your class? Will there be many kids in your class? Will it be difficult to get to know your professor and to seek him out if you have a problem? If it is small, will there be enough courses to choose from? Will there be enough diversity among the students? How big are the dorms? Do they have all the facilities that you want?

Location...how large is the campus? Is it far from an airport? Is it near a large city? How safe is it? Is there transportation on campus? Will you like being far from home? It may be expensive for you to travel home as much as you would like. Will your folks be able to see you often? Right now you may feel it would be awesome to spread your wings and live far from home, but when you really think about it, will you miss your family?

SAT scores and other tests needed...do you have the appropriate scores? Have you taken the right tests to be considered for admission and have you stated that you wish the scores to be sent to the colleges? Other things are taken into consideration besides test scores, but it still is important to be in the ballpark for the SATs.

GPA...what is your average in school? This is the most important aspect of your high school career that is considered by colleges. Have you taken challenging courses? Are your grades at the right level to be considered by the schools you are considering?

Application Deadline...when do you have to submit your application? Make certain you give yourself plenty of time. Keep copies of your application in case the original gets lost. Follow the procedure required not only by the college, but also by your counselor. Make sure your application is done neatly and that you respond accurately to all that is asked.

Fees...if you cannot send in the appropriate fee, you may get a fee waiver from your guidance counselor that will cover the admissions process. Do not let the price of the college keep you from applying; financial aid is available.

Essay...make sure you answer exactly what is asked. If you have an unusual circumstance, make sure you address that. Your essay should be without grammatical mistakes, so make certain that an English teacher proofreads it and gives you appropriate feedback.

Financial Aid...will you be applying for it? Pick up the appropriate forms in Guidance. Some schools want the Profile as well as the FAFSA. Find out the availability of financial aid; are there work-study jobs on campus?

Recommendations ....are they required? How many? Do give the right forms to your teachers and give them enough time to complete them. Choose teachers who know you well and in whose class you have done well. Usually two recommendations, along with one from your guidance counselor, are sufficient.

Majors...are there enough to choose from? Is the one you want available? What do you have to do to fulfill its requirements? Can you go to the school as an undeclared student?

Sports...if you are planning to play Division I or II, have you gone on line to www.NCAAClearinghouse.net and filled out the form? Have you asked your counselor to send in your transcript? Does the school have intramural sports in which you can participate?

Clubs, organizations, student body...what is the make-up of the school? Are fraternities and sororities important? Do you feel comfortable with the types of students you will find on campus? Are students active in organizations?

As you can see, there is much to think about. A good site is www. Collegeboard.com. You will find a lot of information there that will let you sort more easily through the college picking process. Take your time; think about what you really want to do and where you really want to go. It is your future, so plan carefully for it.

***

Judy Cohen

Senioritis

You've heard of bronchitis, sinusitis, and rhinitis...but now we have a new "itis" and it has hit with a bang. Senioritis has invaded and it is very contagious. More and more seniors are coming down with it every day. Actually, its symptoms are easy to recognize.

The student has trouble staying on task with schoolwork. He has a calendar in his room and is busy crossing off the dates until school will be over. She is busy sitting in class, thinking about what to do when school is over, and definitely is not concentrating on the work at hand. He is conjuring up the best way to get out of bed in the morning to come through the hallowed gates of high school when he really does not want to be here. And so it goes.

I am sure you get my drift. Being in high school is not where one wants to be. College, jobs, and the military are looming forth and definitely look more enticing than high school.

Well, now that you know the symptoms, what can be done about treating the disease? In all honesty, not much. Senioritis strikes most students and they have to just push themselves along and try their hardest to stay on task. They have to keep reminding themselves that colleges can rescind their acceptances if their grades really fall down and that colleges do see their final transcript.

So, it is important for them to hang in there. For those who are not going on to college, for those who are going into the military, and for those who are seeking various kinds of jobs, they still need to have that diploma in their hands, so they had better focus to pass courses in order to get the required credits for graduation.

Not only is it hard to concentrate and keep on task as the senior year is winding down, but also the change in the weather does not help. Spring fever exacerbates the problem! With the sun shining and the temperatures climbing, who wants to stay inside and study?

As parents, it is hard to live through this time with your kids. Not only is it hard for them to stay on task, but also they are getting nervous about school ending. Weird, huh? I mean on one hand they cannot wait for school to end; yet on the other hand they are fraught with worry about the next road that they will be traveling. At least they have a safety zone at high school; they feel comfortable, they know the people and the routine.

Even though they want out, change is scary. They really are going through a difficult time and so you, as parents, are going through a hard time, too. Try to be patient. This, too, will pass. Try to encourage them to discuss their feelings with you, although don't be surprised if this is hard to do.

Most teens don't want to discuss things. After all, when you discuss something, it makes it real. Plus, many do not want to display any kind of weakness. They want you to feel that they can handle everything. Perhaps try telling them that you remember senior year and how you felt. By doing this, you are giving them license to speak about their issues. You are letting them know that you have been there and it is normal to feel the way they are feeling. It is normal to have "senioritis".

***

Are All Senior Girls Like This?

Rrring...my phone again. Will it ever stop? Gingerly I lift up the receiver, wary of what I will be hearing. It's been one of those days where staying in bed probably would have been the best option.

After the usual hellos, the voice on the other end woefully asks, "Are all senior girls like this? Do they all drive their folks crazy or is it just mine? Please give me some advice, Mrs. Cohen. Right now, running away seems like a super idea!"

"I can hear that you're upset. What seems to be going on?"

Mom continues by explaining, "She yells at me when I ask her to do something. Clearly she thinks I know nothing; that I am the village idiot. When I try to tell her that I have been around longer than she has and do know a few things, she says, 'Yeah, right!' and clearly means the opposite. If I say white, she says black. If I tell her to study, she has already done so. If I say that I am unhappy with her grades, she claims I am always picking on her. Frankly, I am at my wits end. What has happened to my daughter?"

"You know, this is the second phone call I received today with the same complaint. The actions were a variation on the theme, but the daughter was being just as difficult. I think perhaps I can shed some light for you. At least I may be able to help you understand what is going on. Okay?"

With that I proceed to tell Mom that Sally is going through a difficult time.

"She is now a senior who has a lot on her plate…not just school work and social activities, but deep thoughts such as who am I, where am I going, what am I planning to do. Sally knows that her education at high school is more than half over and she's probably getting a little nervous. She is used to things at high school. What will she find when she ventures forth? Will she be able to handle it? But yet, if you, Mom, keep telling her what to do and how to do it, if you keep getting in her face even though you do because you care, how will she ever become dependent enough to handle things herself? She feels uneasy, but doesn't know how to really voice this uneasiness; instead, she yells at you, Mom, out of fear and frustration. She picks you because you are so close to her. She knows that she can throw barbs your way and you will still have to accept her; you will still be her mom."

After I finish explaining what I thought about Sally's behavior, I then tackle Mom's behavior and feelings. I tell Mom that if she were really to take a good look into herself she may find someone who is a little frightened, too. After all, her once little girl is now blossoming into a grown woman who is about to leave the nest and fly on her own. Yet, Mom really would like to still keep some control of her; Mom is afraid of letting her go.

I don't think it is only because she may be fearful that Sally will not always make good decisions, but rather that she is fearful for herself. Mom will be leaving the comfortable place that she has been in; she will be resigning as conductor of the orchestra and instead will become part of the audience.

"You know," I continued, "this is not an easy time in either of your lives. I still remember when my boys finally went off to college and I wanted to call them every day, yet knew that I shouldn't. I wanted to just hear their voices like I did when they were living at home. I wanted to be a part of their lives. I wanted to know what was going on, whom they were hanging with, what they were doing, how school was going. I wanted to praise them when they excelled, scold them when they didn't and pick them up when they were down."

Mom shook her head in agreement. I could tell she was hanging on to every word.

I went on, "But then I had to stop, I had to put down the receiver and remind myself that they were no longer in my home; I was no longer their guide. I had given them a compass while they were living in my home and hopefully now this inner compass would guide them in the right direction. If not, they would have

166

to learn through their mistakes. The main thing I had to admit to myself was that they were growing up and I couldn't and shouldn't stop the process."

"I understand what you mean, but that is going to be so hard for me to do."

"Yes, but you know, Mom, you will have to grapple with it. Sally is in your home, but she is getting ready to depart and you should help her get ready. Make sure the compass is working. This doesn't mean she has free reign to treat you with disrespect; rather, it means that you both must be respectful of each other. Both of you must share your feelings, be honest with them, and allow each other space. Believe me, Mom, she'll be back and you will love the woman she is in the process of becoming…but that's just it, allow her to make that journey to adulthood."

***

A Senior's Message to Parents

As guidance counselors, we are now hearing from our seniors where they have been accepted and what they are planning to do after graduation. At first, certain about their futures, many are now filled with doubts. Musing about this, I decided to write the following to let you parents in on the turmoil that many of your seniors are feeling.

It's supposed to be fun
A great time in one's life,
Then why is senior year
Filled with such strife?
I try to do my studies
But so much is on my mind,
When I graduate from here
What kind of work will I find?
Or where should I continue
Should I go away or stay near,
And what should be my major
That seems my greatest fear.
Listening to rules, having boundaries,
I think I want to get away,
Now that senior year's almost over
Perhaps I want to stay.
I mean if I go to school closer

I can leave for a home cooked meal,
Or just stop and see my folks
And tell them how I feel.
My thoughts are so confusing
The colleges are letting me know,
But I just can't truly decide
Where it is I wish to go.
I know it will be hard
To leave high school behind,
Not knowing when I venture forth
What I will truly find.
My comfort zone is here
I have friends and family,
Yet when I leave this area
It will all be new to me.
It's difficult to concentrate
On my studies instead,
While all of this stuff
Is circling in my head.
So I may not share this
But things are somewhat scary,
So try to understand
If I seem a little wary.
A big change is going to happen
I hope I don't incur your wrath,
Instead I need your understanding
As I walk this brand new path.
So folks, help me with my future
Be I your daughter or son,
I think I'm all grown-up
But the truth is…I've just begun.

When you think about it, most of the seniors are just 17 or 18 and have had their lives planned for them up until now. So, how do they choose a school? How do they know if they will be happy? How do they know if they really want to go far away from home? How do they know if they really will end up practicing the profession they now think they wish to pursue in college? Will the financial aid be enough? Should they work for a year? Do they want to enter the military? And so the misgivings and musings mount. Believe me, this is not an easy time, so parents, patience and understanding is a virtue.

***

The Road of Life

Wow! Your grade school years are over. Looking back, it seems that they have just flown by. You have learned so much along the way; your friends, your family, your teachers, your books, actually all your experiences, have helped define you and made you who you are today. But you know what, the journey continues so follow along now and see what you will pass along the route and how each sign influences your traveling along the road of life.

You pass a sign for **Curve** in the road. How true of life! Often you just go along and then all of a sudden, you have to change gears and hug the side of the road as you deal with a curve. You pay attention, you go slowly and you find you're able to deal with the curve.

What happens when you come to **Yield**? As in life, you find you often must slow down, and watch how you are progressing. There are other forces around you. You must be cognizant of them and at times proceed slowly.

Sometimes you come to **Merge.** I liken that to compromising. You should be aware of other's needs and wants, take them into consideration and merge with them. At times, it is beneficial to blend in, to dance with others, rather than to dance completely alone to your own tunes.

Put on the brakes! Yes, that's what you have to do when you see **Stop**. How true in life! Sometimes, you just have to put the brakes on, stop yourself from doing or saying something, reassess the situation and then, as it sometimes indicates on the road, **Proceed with caution.**

A sign that may catch your eye is the one that indicates where you can make an **emergency phone call.** As in life, it is important to reach out to others, to communicate when you have a problem, to call someone and to let someone reach out to you in order to help you. When an emergency arises, it is important to seek help in order to deal with it. Often, trying to deal with the emergency alone will not work; you are too close to the problem and unable to see it objectively.

Whenever you see the sign, **Wrong Way,** you may be surprised and wonder why it should be needed, but think about it for a moment. At times, we all do go the wrong way and have to be reminded to regroup, turn around and proceed in the right direction.

No U Turn…that's what looms forth at times, but how many people decide to look around quickly, see if anyone is watching, and then make that prohibited

U-turn? Such is true in life, too. How many times do you make U-turns and keep returning to the problem, rather than going straight ahead and dealing with your life? U-turns cause us to revisit something that we probably should have left behind.

One sign that you may not see too often is the one that tells you that there will be a **Steep Incline**. When you see this sign, you can switch gears, watch the road carefully, and then drive with extra caution. In your life, you will come to times when the going is steep, when the going is difficult, but by switching gears, by proceeding carefully, you should be able to accomplish the climb and finally come out on smooth territory.

Ah, but what about the **Blind Curve**... that one is tough. You really don't see it coming. You have to be able to react appropriately and hang in there. How true of life! Often you do not know what's around the corner, but you have to hold on and deal with any trials and tribulations that may blindly beset you.

Of course, as you drive along, you also hit a lot of smooth driving and that's when the going is easy and enjoyable. Those are the moments in life that you cherish, the ones that allow you to refresh, the ones that allow you to be ready for any of the "highway signs" that will definitely come into view as you continue to travel along your road of life.

The places you will go will be many for your journey is just beginning. May the road you travel be a smooth one; yet, may you be aware of the signposts along the way and have the fortitude, insight, and ability to deal with them.

***

'Twas the Last Day for Seniors

'Twas the last day for Seniors
You could hear a happy cry,
There were smiling faces
But here and there a sigh.
The Seniors were done
But were a little scared, too,
With high school behind them
What now would they do?
Among many of them
There arose quite a clatter,

I got up from my desk
To deal with the matter.
Outside in the hall
Some were stirring about,
"We're happy, but sad,"
I heard one person shout.
"Four years have passed
Now it's time to leave,
I worked hard, I studied
I really did achieve.
I made lots of friends
I found comfort right here,
What's waiting out there
Is what I do fear."
"Come into my office
Is what I want you to do,
Together, I am sure
We will work this thing through."
We sat and we chatted
About the road she would tread,
And told her it was normal
To be filled with some dread.
"Change is difficult, I know
The path will be new,
And some ruts and bumps
Will surely greet you.
But you know, my dear
You are so well prepared,
So have confidence you'll make it
And don't be too scared.
You have a good work ethic
New things you'll explore,
With a positive attitude
I know you will soar."

***

Graduation and Commencement

I know, I know, the title looks redundant, but when you actually consider the two words, you will see that they are different and should both be used to commemorate the important time when one finishes his schooling.

Let's consider the word graduation. It means the completion of a course of study. And that's exactly what is happening to our graduating seniors. They will be done. As the saying goes, "No more teachers, no more books..." Most have worked diligently and will earn their well-deserved diplomas to mark their achievements. But then what?

And that takes me to our next word, commencement. In addition to meaning the time for conferring degrees on candidates, it also means a time of beginning. Indeed, graduation is a time of beginning. It's a time when a student finishes one chapter in his life and begins a new one.

I think it is the idea of commencement that instills fear in a student as well as in his parents. It is the idea of venturing forth into the unknown. After all, the student has been in a comfort zone for 18 plus years; parents usually know where to find him. The student's time is scheduled. He knows when he should get up, when each class begins and ends, when lunch occurs and what his boundaries are concerning parental rules. For 18 years, his educational map has been drawn and defined. There is comfort in that for both student and parent. Now, after 13 years of schooling, that security is about to end and a new beginning, a commencement, is happening.

Having had 3 sons graduate from high school, I know that it can be a difficult time. Yes, I was happy for my sons and proud of their many accomplishments, yet I was unhappy that the apron strings were finally being cut and they were leaving home. I think, too, that the whole happening kind of puts you in touch with the fact that you're getting older; you've reached a new passage.

So, for you as a parent, it's also a time of graduation ...a graduating from being a mom or a dad with a child who comes home for meals, sleeps in the house and lives by your rules, and a time of commencement – a new beginning that requires you to give your kid space, to allow him to go unfettered into the world, learning through his mistakes and accomplishments.

Now that you know it's hard for a parent, can you imagine how hard it is for your child? He doesn't want you to know that he's scared, that he's venturing into the unknown, that he's not sure what he will find or if he will like it. Is he making the right choice? He's been a big man on campus, a football star, a scholar, or whatever, and now he knows he will have to start over again. For him, it's a graduation from his public school to a commencement at a new place.

What can be done to quell this uneasiness on both the parent's and the kid's part? Openness with your feelings is a good way to start. If you admit how you are feeling about his forthcoming graduation, you give your child permission to share his feelings with you. Also, try to share with him how you felt when you finished high school. If you went away to school, what was it like? Honesty is a good way to invite honesty. Getting everything out in the open is a good way to settle that uneasy feeling. Letting your child know that it is normal to have some scary thoughts about graduation will make him feel better.

With kids who are not leaving home, it will still be a change. Routines will be different. They are older now and have to start making their own decisions and by allowing them to do this, you are giving them the wings they need to fly to new heights, to grow, and to explore.

At home, away, at work, and/or at school, do keep the lines of communication open. Set aside time for telephoning and sharing. Send letters and care packages to youngsters who are away. If you reach out, they will reach out and together you will grapple successfully with your new beginning.

As you both, parents and graduates, get used to your new roles, I wish you well. It takes time, but I guarantee, that this next passage will prove to be a rewarding one, filled with challenges, some frustrations, but a lot of satisfaction, too. My best wishes for an enjoyable graduation and a positive commencement.

***

The Commencement Has Begun

Well, the graduation took place and I was very impressed. The students showed decorum; the speakers were excellent; the whole ceremony ran very smoothly. As I stood on the right side of the hall and assisted the students, so many thoughts ran through my mind.

I looked at John and realized how far he had come to reach this moment in time. His home life was difficult, money was scarce, he was father and brother to his siblings, but he had survived. And there he stood, waiting in line to get his diploma. He was visibly beaming and so was I. As he shook my hand, his grip was firm; his eyes were clear. I sensed that John would be fine as he begins his next journey.

There was Erica. She had come such a long way. Initially in remedial classes due to some learning disabilities, Erica went into integrated classes and eventually even took some honors courses. Now she is headed to college. She persevered, she overcame odds, and she succeeded. I am so proud of her and certainly share her excitement and obvious sense of accomplishment.

Then there was Susan, beaming and bubbling. Her family was supportive and intact, she earned good grades, she excelled in sports, and she was well liked by faculty and administration. Clearly, she was "Big Gal on Campus"! As I looked at her, I wondered if all this good fortune had strengthened her, and made her self-assured, or did she need a little seasoning to give her some toughness that would enable her to grapple with life's problems that would invariably arrive?

And so it went. Each young person carried his own story. Some I had read, others I hadn't, but each still touched me, since each was walking forward to graduate and then to commence his or her life as an adult.

Yes commencement – a new beginning. What will it bring to them? As the world turns, what will it hold for them? Will violence cease? Will the economy get better? Will deadly diseases be conquered? So many questions; so few answers. Yet I do know this. Each graduate does have the capability to be all that he can be. Each one has a chance, a new beginning, to forge ahead without the baggage from high school and to start making his way.

Evidently, all the speakers shared my thoughts and delivered them eloquently and passionately in their speeches. For each, in his or her way, spoke about seizing the moment and not dwelling on the past. Each one talked about reaching out, venturing into unknown territory and greeting each day with wonder, zest, strength, and optimism. Hopefully, those words will become ingrained in the listeners and in the speakers. Hopefully, they will use their abilities and work assiduously to make their dreams become realities.

Yes, with graduation the commencement has begun. May the graduates seek and find, listen and hear, reach and obtain, see and understand and risk and gain.

***

Holiday Musings

Thanksgiving

A few years ago, a former student shared with me his feelings of sadness wondering if life simply involved going to work each day, perhaps squeezing in a little bit of fun time with a wife, sports, etc. and then going to bed at night and beginning the whole routine again. To him, it seemed as if a bus were going by quickly and he was standing off to the side, not truly embracing life. He wondered if it got any better.

Immediately, I thought yes, but then I began to let my mind wander back to when I was on the brink of thirty and felt amazingly similar to how he was feeling; the only difference is, I now know why. I had never stopped to smell the roses! I had to make each minute count, but in so doing, I was unable to appreciate any minute and indeed, after a time, began to get burned out.

Every few days, we have to take our cars in to get refueled; yet, we don't allow ourselves time to refuel. We need to stop ourselves, regroup and just think about the beauty around us and the fact that we just ARE. So, one morning, as the water flowed freely in the shower, I let it flow freely over me allowing my mind to stop its frenetic motion. I began to think about the forthcoming holiday of Thanksgiving. Since I equate this holiday with family, I began to think of the family that would be present to share in this wonderful holiday and realized that this is why this holiday is probably my favorite because family, warmth, and love surround me.

Thinking of those who will be seated around the table, I wax sentimental. I ponder the candles with their flames burning brightly and am reminded of the light and brightness that my family has brought into my life. Each, in his or her own way, has left an indelible mark on me and has helped to shape me into the person I am today.

I think of my three sons and how much I have learned from them. From sports, to schoolwork, to relationships, sloppy rooms, fun and laughter, we have shared it all. Yet, how often have I really stopped to appreciate what they have imparted to me? How often have I truly shared with them how much they mean to me? Yes, maybe a hug, a gesture of warmth has shown my feelings, but what have I voiced?

My husband, my helpmate, my soul mate, the one who angers me, cheers me, comforts me, and is just there for me – do I let him know how I feel? Have I shared my thanks and thoughts with him? Have I stopped to truly ponder what he has meant in my life?

And so it goes. I could think the same thoughts, and I do, of parents and siblings. Yet, again, have I shared these thoughts? How many times do I hear in my office when a family member has died, "Mrs. Cohen, if only I had told him how I felt, if only…." But, now it is too late.

After I had spoken to that former student, I decided not to be caught up one day in the "if only". I decided to write down my feelings concerning those who would be gracing my Thanksgiving table and share those feelings at the table. Thinking back, I can still see the flickering flames, and their faces listening so intently to my words. Clearly, they were deeply moved and so was I.

Luckily, I was able to realize how blessed I am and share those feelings. Unfortunately, two years later, one seat around our table was empty. My precious, wonderful dad had died, yet how comforted I was to know that I had shared my feelings with him.

As I look around my Thanksgiving table this year, I know I will feel doubly blessed. My heart will be overflowing with joy. My sons are married to wonderful women and I am blessed with 5 granddaughters. Truly, during this season of the harvest, we are seeing a bumper crop! Our dividends are with us; our happiness is apparent.

Do cherish each one around your Thanksgiving table. Perhaps have each person at the table say why he/she is thankful. Share with others your feelings; let them know how special they are in your life.

***

Tom Turkey Time

How quickly the pages on the calendar turn. It's almost time for ole Tom Turkey to grace our table and I am delighted. I guess it's because Thanksgiving gives me time to pause from my hectic schedule and to contemplate all the reasons I have to be thankful. Most days I am so caught up in my everyday tasks that I really do not stop along the way to think and rejoice in just being.

As I sit at my computer, I muse about my life. It has been a full one so far, filled with sorrows, with joys, with failures and successes. All have added to my tapestry of life; all are an integral part of me. For the good times and the bad times, I am grateful. I have learned from them, I have grown from them. They have helped make me who I am today.

Yes, I am fortunate. My husband is there to greet me when I come home. He listens to my troubles, rejoices in my successes, and nurtures my spirit. But those are things I have come to expect; those are things that I know will happen. Yet, how often do I truly realize how lucky I am that he is there, that he does care, that we have traveled the road of marriage together for almost 40 years, making compromises, muddling through some misunderstandings, yet always regrouping and showing our love and respect for each other?

And what about my sons? Oh how I miss the constant noise and confusion that filled our home as three boys would run through the house, yell messages, play catch in the living room, and drop clothes as they went from room to room. The house was in chaos, but that was okay. It was alive; it was bustling; it was filled with energy. But the boys have moved on. I am so proud of them. They are self-assured, self-sufficient, conscientious and caring. They will always be my children, but now they have taken on the added dimension of friend and for this I am so pleased.

They have married and chosen wonderful women who have become the daughters I never had. Terrific wives, they complement my sons, enrich them, and make them so happy. One son has three daughters; another has two daughters. How beautiful! I hug them; I kiss them. I marvel at their growth, and their achievements. I melt when they call me grandma.

I think of my parents. My precious father is no longer with us, but while he was alive, he was such a presence in my life. I have but to close my eyes and conjure up his image, his handsome visage and booming voice. He is not with me in body, but in spirit and has left me with a legacy of memories for which I am grateful. My mother is now in her 90's. The ravages of old age are taking their toll; I cannot stop the process, yet I can still reach out to her and be thankful for her presence. I can still hold dear the memories that brought us close, that will forever be embedded in my heart.

From family, to work, my mind travels. I realize how lucky I am to work with children who keep me young, who give me so much more than I give them. They nourish my soul; they help me grow in understanding. As I watch them mature over the years, I feel fulfilled. Perhaps I have helped in their growth; perhaps I have positively affected their lives. What could be more rewarding? Even after graduation, some continue to keep in touch, including me in their life cycles, letting me know about their ventures. Yes, as I wax nostalgic about my life, I smile, for I am so fortunate. For life, for freedom, for education, for family, for friends, for health, for love …for all these I give thanks.

As I look around my Thanksgiving table this year, I will be warmed by the faces that surround me, that complete me, define me as a person, and give my life so much meaning.

***

Thanksgiving After the Infamous 9/11 and During the War in Iraq

More than ever, I am looking forward to sitting down with my family, to having them surround me at the table, to looking at them and just being thankful that we are all together.

September 11, 2001 certainly put so many things into perspective. The tangibles are no longer so important to me; the intangibles are what count. I search for and cherish love, caring, hugs, pats on the back, and comforting words. I don't seem to get so upset if I have to wait in line at the supermarket or get caught in traffic. Yes, September 11 gave me a harsh wake up call and made me appreciate things I had taken for granted.

As I was driving to school, I started to muse about the things for which I am thankful.

I am thankful for my husband. He nurtures me, laughs with me, shares my joys and sorrows and rejoices in my being.

I am thankful for my children. I have given them wings and now I am pleased with the flight pattern they have chosen. They are capable, compassionate and able to grapple with the vicissitudes of life. They have chosen wives who complete them as people. I am thankful for these young women, too. They clearly understand my female musings and are the daughters I never had.

I am thankful for my granddaughters who bring such unbridled joy into my life. I hug them, kiss them, play with them, and marvel at their growth and beauty. They are my future.

I am thankful for my job where I feel comfortable. My colleagues are supportive and my students continue to touch my life with their actions and stories. Dealing with them has been so rewarding and has enabled me to grow in understanding and insight.

I am thankful for my country. These past few years "the land of the free and the home of the brave" has certainly rung true. I have never felt more pride in being an American.

I am thankful for my parents who gave me life. No one ever gave them blueprints on how to parent, but they tried their best to instill in me the appropriate tools to enable me to face the world with caring, conviction, courage, and clarity.

I am thankful for the men and women who have fought and will continue to fight to protect our country.

I am thankful for the firefighters and policemen who have shown such strength in adversity and have continuously risen to the challenge.

For life, for liberty, for education, for family, for friends and for the opportunity to exist in a free country, I am forever grateful.

As you sit around your Thanksgiving tables, may you, too, count your blessings and cherish those whom you hold dear. I know you will realize just how precious each one is.

***

Happy Holidays

Yes, it's that time of year again when everyone is supposed to be happy, when Rudolph gets to guide the sleigh, and when Santa comes down the chimney with gifts to make every child's wish come true. It's a time for family gatherings, a time to renew acquaintances, to reach out, to keep in touch, to party, and to celebrate. Yet, not everyone shares in holiday revelry. Not everyone seems to be in a happy mood. Why?

Believe it or not, holiday time is often a time of stress for people. Too often, holidays evoke memories that may be painful. Perhaps Grandpa is not around the table this year. Maybe one's parents have split up and this year Junior will have to divide himself between two households. Father might have a new girlfriend whom

Junior does not like, yet she will be joining in the festivities when all Junior wants is some time alone with Dad whom he has not seen for a while.

Many times, we look back to the previous year and say to ourselves, "What happened to those resolutions we made?" Nothing seems to have changed. Have we failed to make those changes happen? Other times, we may be reluctant to greet the New Year since the old year was good to us and we have no clue what the New Year will bring.

Gina came into my office seemingly depressed. A teacher was concerned about her apparent apathy and gloom in class and had asked me to please see her. She walked in with her head down. She took a seat, but managed to pull it far from my desk. Her hands, although folded in her lap, were moving constantly giving credence to the upheaval that was occurring inside of her.

"Gina," I said in order to establish some eye contact, "How are you doing? I haven't seen you in a while."

She fidgeted a little, then looked up and quickly said, "Fine".

"Are you sure?" I queried and let the question hang in the room.

Slowly Gina lifted her eyes. Still quiet, she seemed to be considering if she should mention her feelings to me.

With my mind trying to fathom the problem, I said, "Perhaps with Christmas coming, this is a tough time of year for you."

You could almost hear a pin drop. Then, it was as if a balloon were being deflated.

She let out a long sigh, her eyes welled up and she quietly said, "You're right."

Gina proceeded to tell me that her Christmases used to be great times until a few years ago when her Grandma had become very ill. She lingered on until just after the holidays and then passed away. Gina still remembered her mom's concern and the somber emotions displayed during that Christmas. The next year, Grandma's death was evoked by her absence at the table and the lack of usual goodies that she would bake.

"I don't know, I seem to be O.K., Mrs. Cohen, but when the holidays approach, I get to thinking about Grandma and I do miss her."

181

I told Gina that her feeling this way was normal; it's what is called an "anniversary".

"You are remembering clearly what happened at the same time a few years ago."

I told her to share some memories of Grandma with me. She smiled, even laughed as she recalled them.

"There," I said, "those are the memories you should hold on to – not the sad ones, but the ones that celebrate Grandma's life, the ones that make her continue to live in your heart. Maybe this year you can even make some of the same goodies that Grandma used to bake."

Yes, holidays can be difficult times, but once we realize why we may be feeling depressed, we can face the depression, deal with it and change our way of viewing the situation. Grandma died, that is sad, but rejoice in all the good memories, recipes, and other things that she bestowed upon you during her life.

To all of you, I wish a holiday season filled with hope, joy, and peace. May the New Year renew your spirit and enable you to fully embrace life remembering your loved ones who have passed on with fondness and cherishing those who grace your life today.

***

Tis the Season to be Merry…Or is it?

The stores are sparkling with shiny decorations, Santa Claus is smiling and voicing his usual "Ho, ho, ho", signs signal sales for the season, and customers are scurrying to pick up the latest bargains. Christmas carols are playing, lights are blinking, and gaiety is in the air. Or is it?

The holiday season has always been one of my favorite times of the year. I think of warmth, I think of comfort, I think of loved ones, I think of caring and sharing. It is a time to reach out to others, to say, "I am here for you." It is a time for people to gather together as a family. It is a time to remember with fond memories those who are no longer with us and to embrace and cherish those who are present. It is a time to exchange gifts – tangible and intangible ones – and to watch the delight on a person's face as he is filled with the pleasure of receiving.

But is this always the case? What about our soldiers overseas? Who will be there for them? Long distance phone calls are a way of reaching out, but what about those enveloping hugs? Those mean so much, yet won't be felt. And what about the homeless? All they desire is a roof over their heads, a roof that belongs to them. To them, the lights of Christmas do not seem to sparkle; they are dulled by the sadness of not having achieved, of not being able to spend time in a home by a fire with family and friends. Perhaps they will go to a soup kitchen and fill their bellies there, but their emotional needs will not be filled.

And what about those who have just recently lost a loved one? The seat at the table will be empty; the requisite phone call will not be received; the peck on the cheek will not be felt. The hearty wishes of the season will not be heard. For those people, the season will be bittersweet. Sweet because of the presence of loved ones and the memories of those who are no longer here, but bitter because of the cruelties of life that have taken people from them. What about those in a Nursing Home with no one left in the family to cheer them? The nurses try, but it is not the same.

Think about presents, too. What about those who cannot afford any? Yes, there is Toy for Joy and other wonderful organizations that provide gifts, but how does the parent feel who cannot provide gifts himself? What happens to his self-esteem? For him, the "ho, ho, ho," does not signify cheer; it signifies failure.

So, although we hear the refrain, "Tis the season to be merry" this is not always the case for everyone. Despair is more prevalent during this season; parents and friends should be on the lookout for depression and reach out to those who are under a veil of gloom. Reach out and lift them up with words, gestures, and perhaps a gift. There are so many ways that you can give. And the intangible gifts...the ones that consist of words of kindness and deeds of caring ...are the most important.

This holiday, be thankful for what you do have and reach out to those who are not so fortunate. Donate a toy for joy, perhaps give some of your time to a food kitchen, purchase a star for a tree, or buy a calling card for someone who is overseas. There are so many ways to give that will truly enrich your lives and make this holiday so much more meaningful. Reach out and you will be surprised how much you will receive.

***

Season of Giving

I was in one of the stores searching for an appropriate gift. A major sale was going on and people were shoving and pushing in order to grab what they wanted. The cash registers could not keep up with the throngs of customers madly waving items in their hands in order to be noticed and waited on. Clearly, the atmosphere was not a cheery one.

As I waited in line, I started to think about this season of giving. Exactly what does this season of giving mean? To begin with, I think some of us have lost sight of the real meaning of the word give. Does it have to mean something tangible? Should it be weighed according to how much the item cost?

I still remember one of the greatest gifts I received. They were green earrings in the shape of dinosaurs. Did I ever wear them? Of course I did and proudly at that. You see, my oldest son had purchased them all by himself. The caring and love that he put into selecting them were forever part of the earrings, so to me the earrings were very, very special. Did they cost a lot monetarily? I doubt it, yet to me, they were worth millions!

Someone once shared the following story with me. Everyone was seated around the Christmas tree busily opening his or her gifts. Smiles came to the faces of the children as they tore open their wrapped gifts and eagerly and happily eyed the contents.

One small child watched with rapt attention as her mother ripped open the envelope that was marked in big letters written in crayon, MOM. Out fell a cut out paper red heart with the words "I Love You" written on it. Underneath was the child's name. A few of the letters were backwards, but it didn't matter.

Through tear filled eyes, the mother looked out at her youngest daughter, smiled and said, "Honey, this is beautiful; I will cherish it always."

Again, it was something that did not cost very much, yet it was invaluable.

Some of the most cherished gifts I have received are cards designed by my students, children and grandchildren, pictures drawn by them, and stories written by them. They did not visit a store to purchase them; instead, they visited their hearts. Yes, gifts from the heart, those are the special ones. Those are the ones that leave their lasting marks on us, that burrow their way into our hearts and fill us with warmth.

Giving - special, meaningful giving – is best when given from the heart. A hug, a kiss, a warm greeting, a visit to the sick or elderly, a batch of cookies made with love…these make such special gifts.

This holiday season, as you enjoy the tangible gifts, do take special note of the intangible ones and embrace them. The gift of family, the gift of love, the gift of caring, the gift of welcome, the gift of friendship, all these gifts and more are truly what the season of giving is about. Cherish these gifts. They are priceless and give lasting meaning to our lives.

***

A Christmas Message

'Twas the week before Christmas
When all through the classes,
Teachers were instructing
All the lads and the lasses.
Some were so attentive
Others listened with one ear,
All were wishing so hard
For vacation to be here.
When all of a sudden
There arose a great clatter,
I rose from my desk
To see what was the matter.
I looked out my door
And what did I see,
A young gal with tears
Looking right back at me.
Into my office she came
It was a short walk,
Sue sat down in a chair
She needed to talk.
"Mrs. Cohen," she said
As she spoke and she sighed,
"I have no Christmas spirit
Last week Grandma died."
When I look at the table
There'll be a blank space,

Where I would have looked
To see Grandma's kind face.
Her cookies won't be there
Her smiles or her touch,
You know, Mrs. Cohen,
I miss her so much."
"Yes, my dear," I replied
"It must be hard to bear,
Grandma won't be around
With you to love and to share."
"But," I continued softly
With a smile on my face,
"Right there in your heart
Will be Grandma's new place.
No one can rob you
Of her essence, my dear,
Close your eyes, remember her
And Grandma will appear.
And as you sit at the table
Among friends and family, too,
There are certain things
That I want you to do.
Look at everyone there
They are so precious to you,
Cherish them, enjoy them
Be grateful for them, Sue.
Find peace this Christmas
May comfort and happiness ensue,
Realize what you do have
And you'll be fine, Sue."
As the day was ending
And I went home that night,
My wish for all of you
Is a Christmas that's bright.
May the burning candles warm you
May your tree stand proud and tall,
Enjoy Christmas with your family
And a Happy New Year to you all.

***

Presence, Not Presents

Now that the holiday season is in full swing, people's thoughts turn to gift giving and mall shopping. I am no exception. The other night, I went to the mall and found the place was jumping! People were discussing what to get for this one and that one. Bargains were being grabbed up and lists were being checked off.

As I was waiting in a long line to purchase several items, I began thinking about the word presents. Then, my mind wandered to the word presence. Yes I know. These two words sound alike, yet they have such different meanings, so I began to think about these homophones and the impact each has on a person's life.

We all do like to receive presents, but are they really the primary things that we want, the things that will bring us the most joy? I don't think so. For the moment we are thrilled with the gift, but that feeling is fleeting.

Think about the child who has a room filled with stuffed animals, perhaps the state-of- the art technology, and the best musical instruments that money can by. Every day, the child goes to her room, plays with the sundry things that she finds there, but doesn't find real enjoyment in them.

What's the problem? The problem is that her folks are away a lot working and when they are home they really don't include her in many of their activities. What she really wants is their presence, not their presents. She wants to feel needed; she wants them there to discuss problems and everyday happenings with her. Simply restated, she wants them around.

Sometimes parents feel that they can "buy" their children's affection. The parents know that they are busy and unable to spend too much time with their offspring, so they feel that presents will make up for their presence. Unfortunately, presents do not communicate. Presents do not give the warmth and nurturing that is needed.

I know it's hard with some people's work to be able to always be present, yet I do feel that parents can make an effort to be present more than sometimes they are. Frankly, I don't think the parents are really aware that their children may need them around more often, since many times, youngsters do not share this feeling with their folks; many times the youngsters are not really aware of why they are feeling so unhappy. Often, the children retreat to their rooms anyway. Other times, they may be aware, but they also know that their parents are working hard and they don't want to upset them and appear selfish by wanting them around. Yet, whether the children are inside of their rooms or not, there is comfort just knowing their parents are home.

I'll never forget going to my sons' athletic games. Many times, I would be exhausted after work, yet I would drive all over to surrounding towns in order to stand and cheer in the cold, wind, hot sun and/or stuffy gymnasium. Looking around, I would often notice children peering into the crowd trying to see if their folks had come to witness their performance. How chagrined they often were to find them absent!

I remember poignantly one encounter with a player. After one of my son's basketball games, the parents came running out on the floor, seeking out their children, and hugging them and praising them. The game had been close, our team had hung in there and victory was ours at last.

I embraced my son, and then looked at the young man next to him. Clearly, no one was there to hug him, so I leaned forward, enveloped him and told him how proud I was of his performance and how lucky my son was to have him as a teammate.

The boy told me that he wished his dad had seen his performance, but it was too difficult for Dad to get to any of his games. How sad! How much the father was missing! Any presents he may have bestowed upon his son would never mean as much to him as his presence.

As you celebrate the holidays with your loved ones, do remember that presents are nice, they are fun to receive and enjoy, but it is presence that is lasting.

***

Resolutions

Yes, it's that time again when we start thinking about resolutions. After all, it's the New Year – a time for new beginnings, a time to take a look back, see what we did not do or what we were unhappy that we did do, and then look for some change in our lives.

Well, we contemplate, we ponder, we question, and we resolve, but do we change? Ah! Will we be able to look back at the end of this year and proudly smile at all we have accomplished? Unfortunately, the answer is more often than not, a resounding NO!

Why is this? We earnestly want to change some aspects so why do we fall short of our goal? Perhaps we reach for the unattainable. Maybe we should reach for something within our grasp, something that is not so hard to attain.

For instance, I remember Mary. She came into my office prior to the Christmas holidays, not sure what to do. Warnings had been issued and she certainly was consistent, having received them in all her major subjects.

"Mrs. Cohen," she said with trepidation, "How can I take these home? But next time, trust me, I will be passing in everything!"

"Whoa, Mary, slow down, let's think this through," I countered, "Let's think about what your grades are in each subject and which ones you realistically think you can raise to a passing grade. Surely it is easier to raise the 50 to passing than the one you currently have a 20 in!"

Realistically…yes, that's the important word. Make sure your resolution is realistic; then it becomes possible and will reward, not frustrate.

To get back to Mary. We decided she should take her warnings home, not make excuses, but rather accept what is and come up with a possible solution. We chose English and Social Studies as courses whose grades could be increased to passing. Through extra help, through constant monitoring, Mary was able to bring up these grades and reap a sense of accomplishment.

We decided, too, that she would not abandon the other courses; she would work hard in them, too, but not expect to bring them up to passing level right away. If she had resolved to pass everything, I think she would have become mired in the mud, so to speak, would have become depressed, would have jumped ship and nothing would have been passed.

Consider another example - many people try to diet for the New Year after enjoying themselves so much during the holidays. Hey, when you play, you often have to pay, but how much? Those who are successful start by setting small goals each week, and then when those goals are reached, they set new ones. In this way, they do not become frustrated and they are able to be successful with their resolution.

At times, it is fun and rewarding to make resolutions with your children. Maybe one of them is overweight and you both decide to lose weight together. At the end of each week, you check in and see what you have lost. In like manner, you may want to give up cigarettes and your child may need to raise his grades. By the end of the marking term, have you begun to cut down? Has your child brought up a few grades? Notice I am not saying that you would have given up cigarettes totally or that all your child's grades are now A's! Spurring each other on, making realistic gains, and rewarding each other with praise, perhaps with a special dinner, often helps resolutions become realities.

So, for all of you out there who are busy making resolutions, do be realistic. Do make some that are within your reach. Otherwise, by the end of the winter, both the ice and your resolutions will have melted!

***

Y2K Arrived and We Survived

Yes, the big Y2K arrived, the fireworks went off at the appropriate times all around the world, and we survived. The computers continued to work, the telephones continued to ring, the lights continued to shine, and the televisions continued to emit their messages. In spite of the hype, the world continued to turn on its axis and we, the inhabitants, are still here to tell the story.

Actually, as I watched the next year ushered in all over the world, I was struck by how we are all tied to this universe, how we all share common feelings of sadness for things lost, joy for things found, and hope for things yet to come. As I saw fathers and mothers celebrating with their children, I thought about the family unit and how it knows no language barrier. Love and caring are the same in any language, in any part of the world.

Each time I picked up a magazine or a paper, I was struck by how many people had made contributions during these past years. Yet, I thought, an important person has been left off of the lists, Every Person. For, indeed, it is every person in his or her own way who has changed the world in some way – some positively, some negatively – but each has done his share to make an impact. When you start to ponder that idea, it makes you realize that each one of us has ownership of this universe and each one of us is important.

Yes, what each attempts to do with his life will either positively or negatively impact the world. In addition, what each chooses to do often has a snowball effect.

For instance, how we treat our children becomes reflected in how they treat their peers and how eventually they treat their own children. How we drive our car may affect the pedestrians and other drivers. How we conduct ourselves at our jobs may affect the raises we receive and in turn affect our family unit. What our children accomplish in school may directly impact their future. It's amazing how many things we affect through our actions.

Remember, each one of us will invariably reap what we sow so let's think about what we wish to sow as we enter the New Year.

As I walked down the aisles in the supermarket, walked around the block or walked down the corridors of the high school, people acknowledged me with a smile and "Happy New Year". I returned the greeting.

Now it's up to each one of us to make that "Happy New Year" not just a greeting, but also a reality. Each of us has the power to apply ourselves assiduously to make that happen. Each of us has the ability for change, growth and contribution. Yes, the New Year arrived and we survived, but let's do more than that. Let's embrace the year, positively affect it, and enjoy the journey.

***

Love

Valentine's Day is almost here. That holiday seems to bring discomfort to some and joy to others. Just why is that? I think it's because the holiday revolves around the word love…a word that is so supercharged with meaning.

Those who do not feel love in their lives certainly do not embrace the holiday. A matter of fact, they enter a store and cringe when they see all the symbols that stand for love…the cards, the cupids, the posters, the hearts…all make them look inward and feel a pang of regret.

Just today I had a girl enter my office.

We started to talk and finally she blurted out, "My dad hates me!"

I looked at her and said, "That's a powerful accusation and a very harsh word…tell me about it."

And she proceeded to do so. Dad is always thinking of himself. He wants, wants and wants. He takes, takes and takes. He never seems to give and this poor gal is feeling starved for affection. She is desperately searching for some sort of praise, even some sort of positive response that she is a decent person, that she is cherished, respected, and wanted. She does not feel she is getting any of this.

"Do you think by acting out in school you are getting back at your dad?"

I left the question hanging in the air, but clearly it needed to be asked. Even maybe subconsciously she wishes to get back at him, but how to do it? Well, if he wants her to succeed, then she will choose not to do so. If he wants her to behave, she will choose to act out. But then whom is she really hurting? I know she left my office with that question humming in her head and I am sure she is contemplating her answer.

I remember another young lady who never really felt loved at home. Unfortunately, she turned to drugs so she would not feel the pain. Eventually, she turned to her boyfriend, too, got pregnant and did have a child. She wanted desperately to love someone and have someone love her in return.

Parents, think to yourselves. Do I tell my child I love him? Do I give him positive vibes when he does something good? Do I show physical signs of affection? Hey, I know it's hard when a son is involved. He just doesn't want to have those pecks on the cheek, but let me tell you, those hugs still feel awfully good. Don't let him kid you about those…just make sure you don't give too many in front of his friends!

I think it is harder for dads to show their love to their kids. They love them desperately, but just are not able to give the requisite hugs. Probably they never received them as kids and are just following learned behavior. Males or females …both need to receive and show love.

Love is so important that when preemies are born, hospitals have people come in to just cuddle and stroke the babies, to show the babies they are loved. They find that these touches of endearment really enable the child to thrive.

Love says, "You are cherished, you are wanted, you are special. I am there for you."

It doesn't have to be voiced all the time; instead, it can be conveyed through actions. However it is communicated, love is important to share, not just during Valentine's Day, but also on every day.

***

Being A Mom

With Mother's Day approaching, I started to give some serious consideration to what being a mom means. Maybe that's why there's a Mother's Day...to give us time to pause, to remember our moms and to do some soul-searching, too.

A mother is thought of as a nurturer. Before a baby is born, Mom houses the child, and gives him physical nourishment. After the baby is born, Mother continues to sustain her child physically by making sure all wants are recognized and met. However, and just as important, a mother must nourish her child emotionally. What an awesome responsibility!

When my children were infants, they would cling to me and hug me. In turn, I would hug and kiss them. I realize how special those times were for me as I snuggled my babies in my arms, as I smelled their sweetness and shared their warmth. As I would give to them, I received so much, too. I was needed, they depended on me, I was loved, and I was hugged. Wow! I felt good! Yes, in giving I reaped so much.

Sure, they were annoying sometimes, they would cry at ungodly hours, they would interrupt my sleep or an important task, but those annoyances would fade in the face of love.

As my boys grew, often a quick hug or a quick peck on the cheek took over for my previous intense hugging and snuggling. I didn't want to embarrass them by too many outward displays of emotion. When I did, I would see them looking around to see if someone else saw what I was doing. Why did my emotional response towards them have to change since inwardly I felt just the same? Ah, they did, too, I'm sure, but it wasn't cool to let others know that. So, I would articulate my feelings; with words I would let them know how special they are. I gave them pats on the back showing praise and encouragement. I sneaked in a hug or two to show support.

After all, I am a mom and the caring doesn't stop. I do find that the worrying grows as they do. My grandmother used to say, "Little children, little problems; big children, bigger problems". How wise and accurate she was. But even in spite of the pitfalls, even in spite of a few rough spots, love smoothes them out and prevails.

My boys left for college. I knew they were growing away from me and asserting their independence, yet the emotional bond of love still bound us together.

I welcomed the opportunity to let them attend college, yet I found it so hard to say goodbye.

As they walked off toward their new home, I truly felt I had a hole in my heart. Yet, I had to show them my love by letting them go, by having confidence in them that they would survive, that I had given them tools such as insight, warmth, love and coping skills that would help them succeed.

Now, my sons are married. I find my love is shared by another. I don't want to intrude, yet I want them to know how I feel, how precious they are to me, how they define me as a mom and give my life added meaning. Yet, the involvement isn't the same and I miss that. I am still a mom and they are still my sons, yet they have added the role of husband and I must give them space.

Two of my sons are living far from home. The hugging must be done over the phone. I miss the physical contact; I have to settle for shared words, for utterances of endearment until the next trip when we see each other. I find I telephone often.

Now, I have granddaughters, so I am a mom and grandma. How sweet, how beautiful, how special! The intense hugging and snuggling begins again. I am ecstatic. The saying, "My cup runneth over" is so true. One only has to observe me as I hug my granddaughters, give them kisses, and glow when they smile back at me.

I am content. I have been given the gifts of motherhood and grandmotherhood. I cherish them, recognize their inherent responsibilities and rejoice in their roles.

To all you mothers out there, reach out, give hugs, and each child, according to his personality, will respond to your warmth.

***

A Mother's Day Message

The stores and the newspapers are shouting out at everyone, "It's Mother's Day...remember your mom". As I looked at the ads and read the signs, I began to muse about my mother, myself, and about all moms in general.

Among my thoughts, one very interesting one kept surfacing and needed to be examined more closely - the definition of motherhood. Exactly what does make a mother? Does one have to give birth to be called a mom?

Without mulling that over for more than a nanosecond, I came up with a resounding, "No!" All I have to do is think about some women who have given birth and then do not care for their children. Conversely, I think about those who have not been birth mothers, yet are the best mothers one could possibly find.

Why? Let me explain. A mother is a woman who is able to nurture. She gives of herself freely, wrapping herself in the concerns of another. She is there to listen, to advise, to take care of physical and mental wants. She is there to lift up when one falls and to rejoice when one rises. She is a mentor, a philosopher, a doctor, a nurse, a cook, and a cleaner. She straightens rooms and helps straighten lives.

I look at my niece. Unable to carry a child of her own, she adopted one. She gave the supreme gift, the gift of a good life to a child who would not have had one. She rescued an abandoned child and now is nurturing her as if she were biologically hers. It is a miracle for both. The child and my niece are completed as people. It is a symbiotic bond, with each growing from the other. This beautiful child with the dancing eyes could not be any more my niece's child. The warmth that is emitted from their togetherness is palpable. Their smiles, hugs, and kisses say it all.

I look to others who have taken in children at various stages of development. They have done so willingly, knowing that by positively touching someone else's life they will forever positively touch their own. What greater gift is there than that? They reach out and give, not just in material ways, but also more importantly, in intangible, unmeasured ways.

Often, having another enter a household is not easy, but they hold on, clinging to the knowledge that they will make a difference. They are selfless in their devotion to make the newcomer feel whole and included. Love, caring, and sharing bind them inextricably to one another.

Of course, the moms who are blessed with being birth moms must be recognized, too. There is beauty in giving birth, in creating life, in being responsible for another human being, in being able to allow the generations to continue beating strongly.

But, just because they give birth, are they good moms? Not necessarily. Don't get me wrong. Many are, but some are not. Perhaps because of other circumstances beyond their control, perhaps because of their own upbringings, perhaps because of many other issues, they are not able to truly reach out and nurture. Many of them do not know how. They have not been nurtured, they have not been loved and therefore, they react in a similar fashion.

Unfortunately, there is not really a blueprint for mothering. One really learns as one progresses. I think first kids have it the hardest because of this. We are learning on them and with them, but the important thing is that we do learn. From every situation we learn. As our children thrive, we thrive. As our children grow, we grow.

To me, motherhood is the most important job in the world. It is fraught with frustration, it is fraught with anxiety, it is fraught with anger and sorrow, but it is so filled with love, tenderness, enjoyment and hope.

It is filled with wonder, and that I think makes it so special. It is filled with the wonder of seeing a child unfold, of seeing a child crawl, then walk, and eventually run down the path of life, secure, with joy on his face, and love in his heart.

And even as he matures and grows into an upstanding young man, he will still be your child. And when the phone rings and you hear his voice, you will still get a warm feeling in your heart. When he enters a room, your face will crease into a wide smile. You will envelop him warmly. Your spirit soars. And when he says, "I love you," there needs to be no response. Those words and the hug you return say it all.

To all you moms out there…biological or surrogate…I wish you a very happy Mother's Day. Your job is such an important one, and such a wonderful one, too. You have been given the gift of motherhood. Embrace it and cherish it.

***

A Father's Day Message

Often I am behind a car that has a bumper sticker that asks the question, "Have you hugged your child today?" Each time it gives me pause and I begin to muse just how important it is to show your child affection, to let him know not just with words how special he is to you.

I still remember the time a young man came into my office and was very upset with his father. It seems they just never got along. Dad had remarried, had children with his new wife and this boy, his son, felt slighted, unwanted, and hurt. Yet, did Dad know this? Had his son shared his feelings with Dad? Through conversation, I learned that Dad did not really know his son's feelings; a matter of fact, both never communicated that much.

A telephone call was made. Dad came into my office the next morning. The son was there, too. Always noticing body language, I was struck by theirs. Dad took a chair and moved it to one side of my office; his son took a chair and moved it to the other side. There they sat, separated like two islands. We spoke for a while and I elicited responses from each one.

Finally, noticing the lack of eye contact that each had for the other, I asked the young man, "Does Dad ever hug you? Does he ever put his arms around you and tell you how much you mean to him?"

He squirmed in his chair, shook his leg, put his head down, and then I noticed that his shoulders were shaking.

With tears streaming down his face, he looked up at me and quietly said, "No".

I glanced at Dad who had begun fidgeting and was clearly agitated. A large man, he suddenly looked small to me.

With pain written on his face, Dad said in a subdued tone, "I had no idea my son was feeling this way. I do hug the girls, but my own folks never hugged me, just my sisters, so I guess I just never thought about hugging my son."

And then with a catch in his voice, he looked over at his son and simply said, "I'm sorry."

I waited, glued in my seat. It was so quiet I could hear the clock ticking. Dad looked at his son; his son looked at him. Dad slowly arose from his chair, walked over to his son, and put his arms around his son. Holding his son tightly, Dad felt his son returning the hug. Both had tears in their eyes, but they were tears from feeling good.

After that meeting, I am happy to say, things dramatically improved. The boy realized that Dad loved him as much as he loved his half-sisters, even though he had never visibly shown it or verbally expressed it. Both learned how important it is to communicate feelings, to actually show how you feel. Often, a good hug is worth a thousand words.

On Father's Day, or any day for that matter, you fathers out there, do some soul searching. Have you shown your kids how much they mean to you? Have you, through your actions, invited them to show you how they are feeling, or, through your aloofness, have you kept them at arm's length?

Children need to know that they are loved; it is not a sign of weakness for you to do this. So I ask you to think about this. Have YOU hugged your child today? Years ago, in my office, Dad and his son did and what a difference it has made!

***

Fatherhood

Walking into a card store, I notice all types of cards for dads. Yes, it's that time of year again. Father's Day is fast approaching. But the thought of the day gives me pause. Just what does make a father? Is it the person who fathered the child? Not necessarily. It is only that person if he is the one who nurtures the child, who unquestionably loves the child, who reaches out to the child with warmth and words.

Being a dad is an awesome responsibility. One has to be a doctor, a teacher, a friend, a role model, a disciplinarian, and a haven. Wow…so many hats to wear!

Dads, you often have difficulty showing emotions. After all, it is not manly to cry. It is not manly to show your feelings. But is this healthy? What are you showing your children? Don't you want them to feel? Only through reaching out to your children will they learn to reach out to others. They need to learn what a hug feels like. They need to hear the words, "I love you."

The following deals with fathers and sons, but many of the same issues hold true with dads and daughters.

Children need your guidance. They want it; they yearn for it. But they do not want guidance bestowed in a negative way. They need constructive comments, not destructive ones. It's okay to tell them they are wrong, but tell them why they are wrong and what they can do to improve.

Many times dads leave the lessons of life to moms, but when they do this, they are missing out on so much. Only through sharing, talking, and caring will bonding ensue. Only then will communications take place and closeness become a reality.

My sons are grown but my husband still picks up the phone and calls them regularly. I can hear laughter, encouragement, and advice being shared. When they see each other, not only words are exchanged, but also hugs are given. How beautiful! How meaningful!

When I look at two of my sons who are fathers, I marvel. So deftly do they deal with their children. With obvious delight, they interact with them, tossing them in the air, reading them stories, teaching them songs, and yes, disciplining them, too.

But the disciplining is done with love. Even with their young children, a no is given with a reason that clearly adds meaning and rightness to the no. Through their interactions, they are teaching their children how to behave. They are role models; they are the ones their children will emulate.

Together with his spouse, each dad has been given a piece of clay and has been granted the awesome task of molding it. What shape will the clay become? What imprints will be made? Whatever marks Dad makes on the clay will be there for a lifetime. Some marks will fade a little in time, but each one will become a spot on the fabric of the child's life, helping to determine what the child will grapple with as he progresses through life. Hopefully, the marks will include the tools of insight, love, understanding, and coping that will enable the child to be successful.

Dads, it is important for you to look inward. Who are you? Where are you going? What do you want for your child? When you are secure within yourself, you will be secure reaching out to your child. Take what you have learned from your folks. Use what has worked. Leave behind what hasn't, making a determined and conscious decision to be the kind of dad that you wanted or had.

You will be helping your son grow from baby to boy to man. When he is an infant, you are one of the people who will be responsible for his every need. You will bathe him, change him, kiss him, hug him, play peek-a-boo with him and marvel at his responses.

As he grows into a boy, make sure the hugging continues. The talks will be more directive with more teaching involved. Go with him to his games. Be there with him as he learns new things. Encourage him to interact with others and then give him the license to move on. But never stop outwardly showing your love for him.

Yes, he will probably be embarrassed if you give him a big sloppy kiss, so try a hug and a quick peck instead. Keep giving him signs to show him he is important. Give him space to grow, but give him boundaries, too. He will be exploring new territories, but help him to know which ones are appropriate and which ones are safe.

In just a blink of the eye, you will notice that this little lad has grown from boy to man. He has grown in understanding and stature. He has taken what you have given him and is walking with determination and confidence.

You will notice that you will be walking side by side, not in front or behind each other. And you will look at him, as I do at my sons, and be filled with warmth and pride. You will be proud of all that he has become.

In turn, he will look at you, smile, and inwardly give thanks that you have been and will continue to be a dad in the truest sense of the word.

***

About the Author

Judy Cohen, born and raised in Massachusetts, earned an undergraduate degree in education and a graduate degree in guidance and psychological services. Ms. Cohen contributes to a local newspaper by writing timely articles concerning her interaction with her own family, students, their family and the staff at her high school. As a mother of three sons, she has been fully immersed in the parenting role. She has spent thirty years in education - teaching, tutoring and counseling. Through her work, she has gained invaluable insights toward helping herself and others work through difficult times and has developed a deeper understanding into the feelings and actions of adolescents and their families. She lives in Massachusetts with her husband, Michael, and dog, Stanley.

Printed in the United States
25629LVS00004BA/139-204

What the Guidance Counselor has Learned

I've learned how much I have gained and grown from being a guidance counselor.
I've learned that each child I have known has touched me in so many ways.
I've learned that putting my thoughts down on paper and writing this book have given me pause and taught me so much.
I've learned that counting to 10 helps, but counting to 20 is even better.
I've learned that sometimes you have to walk through valleys in order to reach mountains.
I've learned that keeping an open mind allows new ideas to enter.
I've learned when one door closes, invariably another one opens.
I've learned when a door opens, it is important to walk through it.
I've learned to shuffle the cards of life and look at them in different ways.
I've learned to try to sweat only the big stuff.
I've learned to listen more and speak less.
I've learned to hear the sounds of body language for therein often lies the truth.
I've learned to marvel at the rising of the sun and realize a new day is dawning.
I've learned to count my blessings, not my failures.
I've learned to embrace life and squeeze it to its fullest.
I've leaned to look beneath the cover of things and make wonderful discoveries.
I've learned that reaching out enables one to receive.
I've learned that the love of family warms the heart and comforts the spirit.
I've learned the beauty of grandchildren.
I've learned it's important to sow the seeds in order to reap the harvest.
I've learned that friendship is like a big hug.
I've learned to look at the road ahead, not at the one behind me.
I've learned that each experience has meaning and adds to the fabric of my being.
I've learned how important it is to keep learning.

***

Conclusion